How to Win Friends and Influence Profits

The art of winning more business from your clients

David Kean & Chris Cowpe

Marshall Cavendish
Business

First published in 2008 by:

Marshall Cavendish Limited
Fifth Floor
32–38 Saffron Hill
London EC1N 8FH
United Kingdom
T: +44 (0)20 7421 8120
F: +44 (0)20 7421 8121
sales@marshallcavendish.co.uk
www.marshallcavendish.co.uk

A CIP record for this book is available from the British Library

ISBN-13: 978-1-905736-19-5
ISBN-10: 1-905736-19-3

Printed and bound in the UK by
CPI Mackays, Chatham ME5 8TD

Acknowledgements

There are four groups of people to whom we would like to say a very big thank you. Firstly, our clients – all of them, old and new. This book is about what we have learnt working with you. Secondly, our colleagues over the years, who have been so liberal with their own views on what is good and what is bad practice. This book borrows heavily on your wisdom and experience. Thirdly, the lawyers, bankers, architects, consultants, headhunters, advertisers, marketers, auditors, accountants and other professionals who very kindly allowed us to cite their experiences for our case studies. This book gets much of its down-to-earth practicality from their trials and tribulations. And lastly, all our friends who have read our words, shouted encouragement from the sidelines and made the book immeasurably better with their thoughts and suggestions.

Dedication

We have dedicated this book to Dale Carnegie because we believe he wrote the finest textbook on business practice ever written. In truth, all other business books have been but a footnote to his seminal work *How to Win Friends and Influence People*. Our book is, we hope, in the spirit of his philosophy, and we chose the title in homage to the great man. Yes, we've given it a more obviously commercial title in line with the specific remit we've given ourselves: how to win more business from the clients you already have. But we hope and believe he would recognize and approve of our approach.

Similarly, Carnegie wrote his book as an "action" book – one designed to give people ideas that they could put into practice immediately. We, too, hope that this book stimulates you to take action, so that you can develop stronger, deeper relationships with your clients.

Everything this book covers is based on experience: our own experience working in and with professional service organizations over the last three decades, learning from the experience of others and talking – talking to as many people as possible about our ideas, hypotheses and solutions. We hope you find it stimulating. So stimulating you actually use it!

Contents

Definitions

We use two phrases throughout this book which we want to define:

Organic growth: means the additional assignments or mandates and therefore income and fees a professional service company can gain from its existing clients. This is sometimes called farming or cross-selling. It therefore excludes growth by, for example, merger, acquisition or financial engineering. Specifically, we distinguish between organic growth and what we call new business – which means assignments from clients with whom a professional service company does *not* have either an existing or at least a recent relationship.

Existing client: for us, a client implies either a corporate or an individual relationship and we use the term in both senses. There are incredibly strong relationships between the corporate entities of client companies and their professional service partners; but equally so between individuals within organizations and sometimes between individuals and organizations.

But we recognize that the term "existing client" has a degree of ambiguity. We use a simple formula that helps us to define what an "existing client" means:

Recency × significance × intensity × contact = existing client.

If you are working today with a client on a project of huge importance to them or their company at a level of intimacy where personal or corporate confidences are shared, and you are in contact consistently and personally, that is *definitely* an existing client! Change any of these parameters and you will have to be your own judge of the extent to which the relationship can or cannot be described as existing.

Taking organic growth seriously

Most companies devote huge amounts of energy, time and resources to bringing in new clients or acquiring companies in their relentless ambition to grow and to satisfy investor demands. Mergers and acquisitions (M&As) and winning new clients are the rock 'n' roll of the business world: exciting, dynamic and sexy. By comparison, growing revenues from existing clients tends to be outshone by these more glamorous stepsisters. And yet in survey after survey within professional services industries, those companies that grew organically had much higher shareholder returns than those that grew through acquisitions.

This first section looks at why it is time for all professional services companies to take organic growth much more seriously. By holding up a mirror to how people behave in the real world, where lip-service is all too often paid to the need for organic growth but without the organizational commitment to *really* making it happen, we want to remind the business world of this basic truth: **"It's about your clients, stupid!"** (with apologies to Bill Clinton).

1

Organic growth: finding Cinderella in every professional services firm

The single biggest imperative for all business organizations is growth. Profitable growth. Growth can be achieved in a number of different ways: through acquisition or merger, winning new clients or winning more business from existing clients. But not all growth is created equal – at least not according to the stock market. Organic growth, sustainable and profitable top-line growth, is highly prized and rewarded better in the financial markets.

A study within the life insurance industry, by Deloitte Consulting LLP, analysed the revenue performance and shareholder returns of the top companies between 2001 and 2005. Those companies that grew organically had much higher shareholder returns than those that grew through acquisitions – even when their revenue growth was smaller than that of their acquisition-driven competitors. They had an average shareholder return over the period of 11% on an average revenue growth of 7% versus a negative average shareholder return in those companies fuelled by acquisition.

Increasingly, organic growth is seen as a vital driver of business performance across many professional services organizations. A number of studies over the last few years have demonstrated this, such as the management consultancy A. T. Kearney's Financial Institutions Organic Growth Index, which stated in 2005: "to achieve superior shareholder value, financial institutions must achieve organic growth rates of at least 6 to 8 per cent annually." Similarly, Rydex Investment's 2006 Adviser Benchmarking Survey on financial advisers demonstrates that the best-performing firms produced revenues per client of almost four times those of average firms in the sector. The survey also shows a marked disparity in the annualized client attrition figures of the best performing firms (3% of clients lost) versus the average (15% of clients lost).

And yet, in that same study, only 34% of the financial advisers surveyed felt that client retention and development are important measurements for evaluating the performance of their business. Despite the vital importance of organic growth it simply is not on everyone's radar in the way it should be.

We've worked in the professional services sector for a long time. And we thought that a simple, straightforward, practical handbook showing professional services companies how best to get more business from their existing clients was long overdue.

The book is aimed at investment bankers, lawyers, architects, accountants, advertising agencies, financial analysts and advisers, business consultants – in fact, anyone who has a portfolio of existing clients and the opportunity to grow business with those clients. And despite the fact that organic growth is a key driver of company profitability there is little literature or guidance on the subject, and even fewer case studies. Our aim is to shed light on this neglected subject:

> Why it's important to companies in terms of revenue, profit margin and their future success.

> Why it is often neglected because of silo mentalities, ego, the distractions of day-to-day delivery and the greater sexiness of new business.

> How companies and individuals can undertake a more systematic approach to developing the key skills that unlock organic growth potential and lead to huge competitive advantage.

And although the book is aimed at professionals, we've deliberately drawn on a wide variety of examples to illustrate how really good practitioners of organic growth achieve spectacular results. We've used the experiences of professional service firms, of individuals we admire in all walks of business life and even from greengrocers!

If you think there's a limit to what can be learned from a humble fruit-and-veg stallholder, just remember that greengrocers have a nasty habit of being quite successful – Tesco, Marks and Spencer, Sainsbury – so they really are a good role model. Indeed, some of our stallholders' skills are still clearly in evidence with these large organizations: Tesco champion good value and quality, have introduced a breadth and depth of products that make the weekly shop stimulating and rewarding, go out of their way to

The Greengrocer

Let's start with the basics and take a fruit-and-vegetable stallholder in a street market. Does he know the secret of getting his customers to come back again and again? Absolutely! To start with he'll remind his customers he's there, advertising his quality produce and unbeatable value, by shouting out to passers-by at great volume. He'll make the experience of dealing with him fun, lively and entertaining. There will always be plenty of banter. He'll use some outlandish analogies to describe just how wonderful his produce is. All his wares are on display, looking magnificent – shiny and attractively presented. They will be clearly labelled and there will always be some special offer on a particular item to help bring you to his stall.

And once you do approach his pitch, he'll encourage you to interact with him and to touch and feel his merchandise. He's drawing you in, getting you to commit by increasing your sense of appetite and obligation. He'll engage you in direct conversation and get you to try one of his juicy, fresh-off-the-boat, seedless grapes. You're drawn in more. He'll ask you some questions: what are you looking for? You ask for apples.

" Red ones, green ones, cooking ones, organic ones, big ones, small ones?" he asks.

"Organic ones please," you reply.

So you buy some apples – some organic ones and a few small ones of an unusual variety.

But do you walk away only with some apples? No way. He'll get you to try a slice of kiwi fruit and get you to feel the weight of his juice-laden Seville oranges (notice how he uses evocative language to add value to the commodities he's selling – Seville oranges, renowned as the best, most juicy oranges in the world; peerless South African pears; organic, seedless grapes from the Cape; dates from the Lebanon, where the world's finest are cultivated) which you will then buy. You will walk away weighed down with two or three times the amount of fruit you intended to buy.

Will you resent this gross abuse of your funds? Not a bit of it, for aside from buying his excellent produce you have had five minutes' banter, a lively and educative conversation – during which he probably gave you a recipe idea to stimulate your creativity – and a memorable experience, a mini-event in your daily routine.

Will you go back next week? Of course you will. Because he provided all the ingredients that make a highly profitable relationship for him and an enriching experience for you. And the more you go back, the more he'll find out about you, your family, your likes and dislikes, and the more he'll be able to tailor his weekly five minutes with you until they're ten minutes or more and you genuinely look forward to your conversation with him. And all you wanted was an apple.

be as available as possible – whether out of town, on the high street or at your front door – know you and their other millions of customers intimately through their ClubCard, and have encapsulated their philosophy in three powerful words: Every Little Helps.

Greengrocers and other tradespeople have been passing the key skills we talk about in this book down from father to son, mother to daughter, for generations. Why? Because these skills grow existing client relationships and unlock sales and profits faster than any other talent you can acquire. These people are worth studying.

What can we learn? Like most professional services companies, they don't know much about their customers to start with, but through polite curiosity and a bit of conversation they glean lots of useful information – *so that they can help their customers better.* They guide you through the range of their offerings. They let you try some of their merchandise – with no financial commitment from you. They ensure that their brief time with you is memorable for all the right reasons. They will make you go on your way with a smile on your face, having lightened the load a little. Every week they will have something new to show you. They will remember what you bought from them last time and enquire with genuine interest how you used it (did you make that fruit flan?) and whether you enjoyed it. They will always be interested in you and what you have to say.

And you will become a loyal customer of theirs – not only that, but you will also tell all your friends and neighbours about this stall and so provide the stallholder with testimonials and referral business. You will become an unpaid apostle for them, and you won't begrudge it one iota. Because this stallholder has become not only your trusted fruit adviser, but part of your personal landscape, a person with whom you are happy to while away a bit of time and trade conversation.

Organic growth is easy – there are great examples of it all around, if only you keep your eyes, ears and minds open!

2
Why organic growth is so valuable

Most people working in professional service firms intuitively know and believe that developing more business from their existing client base is desirable. They are certainly not going to argue against it. But it is vitally important not just to think of it as desirable, but to be able to understand and clearly articulate the case for organic growth; because unless there is a clearer appreciation of just how valuable it is, belief will remain hazy, commitment low and action vague and imprecise. Knowing is believing, believing is acting.

The basic – and what can be more basic than money? – argument for organic growth is that it is more profitable and higher-margin than gaining new business from new clients. New revenues from existing clients often drop a larger percentage of the incremental spend to the firm's bottom line than new-client wins.

There are a number of commonsense reasons for this.

> Existing teams are already in place and can often absorb some if not all of the increased workload,

despite the protestations that "everyone is far too busy these days to do more"; in reality more people *can* do more given the opportunity.

> If new people are required on the team, it is possible – even desirable – to introduce more junior staff into an established relationship. Possible because the relationship and trust between client and firm already exist, so allowing younger people to grow into new roles; and desirable because every professional service company should be wanting to provide new opportunities for their employees.

> The start-up costs associated with new clients devour time and resources as the team gets up to speed with their business, their market and their modus operandi. Over-servicing a new client in the early months is mandatory and important and should build a longer-term relationship, but it is undoubtedly expensive.

> Given that a relationship already exists, it is often the case that organic assignments are non-competitive; and given that the odds of winning new business are at best one in four – and often far worse – then there is more probability of the mandate being realized.

> Many of the uncertainties that crop up with a new client can be more surely and swiftly resolved. For example, new-client assignments sometimes fail to materialize on the scale promised and then suffer a lingering death, with both sides unable to admit that the promised land was in fact a mirage. This is far less likely to happen or can be resolved more promptly within a relationship where both parties already know and trust one another.

Overall, there are powerful and compelling financial reasons why organic growth is of greater value to a professional service firm in most situations than its new-business equivalent.

And there are other important reasons why it is of great value to the future prosperity of every professional service firm.

1 **Gaining business from existing clients is the ultimate quality reassurance** to all current and prospective stakeholders – clients, employees, shareholders – of your company's abilities. If you were a client putting your business up for pitch and you visited a group of potential professional advisers to help you decide which you wanted to appoint, who would you be more impressed with?

COMPANY ABC, who show in their credentials presentation that they have won 75% of the new-business pitches they have competed in over the last year (or have offices in 75% of the known cities in the world, or 75% of their employees have degrees, or 75% of ...)?

COMPANY XYZ, who have been awarded additional business by 75% of their existing clients over the last year?

Company XYZ is going to win hands down.

It is so much more convincing, and it sends such a reassuring signal to prospective clients, to know that your company is being rewarded by those with whom you already have assignments. There is no finer compliment a client can give you than to award you another slice of their pie. It is the best evidence that they believe you are doing a great job for their business.

And it is also a truly powerful reward for the firm's employees. It means that their expertise and advice have merited further commissions from a satisfied client.

2   **Successful organic growth means that you have a broader and deeper relationship** with your client, thus improving the stickiness of the relationship. You now have two not one, three not two connections ... and these increased interdependencies mean that you are better able to provide sounder advice and recommendations across a wider canvas, have a broader, deeper relationship with the company and more individual clients, and therefore a greater hold on their business. This is a real win-win situation. Your client gets better advice because you are able to see and understand more of their business; you achieve the benefits of increased revenues and a greater loyalty factor.

3   **Organic growth means being proactive**. Every company has to have clients in order to thrive. And every company has competitors trying to seduce those clients away. This book is one of the surest ways to fireproof your business against client defection, because being aware of a client's business needs, offering new ideas, helping change or improve processes are what any client wants from his professional advisers – and if you're not providing these things, someone else will.

4   **Finally, without organic growth the value of many new-business wins is hugely diminished.** Most professional firms will take on small and sometimes

unprofitable clients *provided* they believe that winning this assignment will unlock the door to larger and more lucrative assignments in the future.

You may recognize this argument:

"OK, I know this project is only worth $100,000; and yes, it may cost us money in the short term. But that's a very narrow definition of what this project is really about and what it could mean to us. This company spends $10 million on the types of services that we provide. That's the real prize that we're pitching for – so, let's do it."

And of course, when the argument is put like that, the firm redoubles its efforts – and time and expenditure and senior partner commitment – to win not the $100,000 prize but the theoretical one that is a hundred times bigger.

The logic in this approach is impeccable. Small projects can and do lead to other bigger mandates; and if this is likely, it's right to throw disproportionate resources at the pitch. But this is valid only if the firm has a powerful and successful strategy to unlock some of that $10 million. Otherwise the whole exercise is pointlessly wasteful. The value of many new business wins can be unlocked only if an organic growth strategy is in place.

Case studies: an explanatory note

We have included specific examples from a wide spectrum of professional service companies. The case studies are real-life examples of putting theory into practice. They are intended to stimulate, provoke and to give ideas. They are the experiences of practitioners. They describe a situation, the issues and their resolution, the achievements made and those challenges still remaining.

We asked three basic questions:

> Why is organic growth important to you and your company?

> What are the barriers to achieving organic growth?

> What have you done to achieve success?

We made the decision to publish our case studies anonymously. We wanted people to tell their story, not give us propaganda; to talk about the difficulties, not just the successes. We also believe that everyone can learn from everyone else – the banker's tale should be of relevance to a management consultant, the consultant's to a lawyer, and so on – because the learning lies in the stories: it's not just about being right or wrong but about the thinking and the approach to the issues we all face in service businesses.

But our most important reason for disguising our case conversations was that everyone to whom we spoke believed that their approach provided them with some level of competitive advantage. They know that they may not have the total solution, but they believe that how they do what they do is distinctive and valuable. They would not talk without the security of discretion. We agree. In the world of professional service organizations, how you do things is as important as what you do and the how is often the competitive advantage.

So the case conversations have been disguised – names and dates have been changed, locations amended, sector-specific jargon eradicated – but they are true to the spirit of our conversation.

The banker's tale

Steve is the managing director of one of the major divisions of BankCo, a European investment bank. In a sense, his job is entirely defined by his ability to build relations with his clients in order to maximize BankCo's share of their transactions. For him the issue is not the merits or otherwise of organic growth but simply how successful they are at delivering it.

"We will often embark on a new relationship knowing that initially it will be a loss leader. The deal is not judged over the short term, but on whether the bank can recoup that initial loss and grow revenues over the mid to long term."

Like so many others, he regards the quality and depth of his client relationships as the vital foundation stone of success. Relationships need "to be able to survive and flourish in the bad times as well as the good", "to be personal without being obtrusive" and "to be open enough so that conversations can be about problem/solutions, not a blunt product-based approach."

But BankCo has a particular approach to building excellent client relations, having decided that they will not be an all-purpose, universal investment bank. Strategically, they have decided to focus on a small number of key product lines. And they tell their clients overtly and forcefully that this is what they do and that their ambition is to maximize their mandates in these specific areas.

"We are quite clear with our clients. We tell them that we

expect to be at the top of their shortlist if there's a deal in our areas of focus. It may sound curious but our clients appreciate this – they know what we do, they know that we are totally credible in and committed to these areas, and they know what our ambitions are – and what they are not! The relationship is definitely strengthened by having this clarity and transparency; at the end of the day we both know where we stand with one another."

Given that relationships are at the heart of BankCo's growth strategy, the principal challenge faced by Steve and his colleagues is how they can maintain the necessary breadth and depth of relationships in a fast-changing world. Companies change through takeovers and mergers, individuals change through promotion or job moves. And clients themselves have to manage their banking relationships. Clients need a roster of banks to serve different geographies and different financial needs, among whom they share transactions and mandates.

In terms of achieving their objectives, BankCo has a number of supporting processes and principles.

Like many other international service organizations they have a client structure headed by a global relationship manager, who controls and orchestrates the client relationship. "They have to know everyone and everything – from the mortgage in Kenya to the acquisition in Germany."

This structure is supported by a recently introduced Management Information System (MIS) replacing the more ad hoc system that had evolved piecemeal over many years.

"This allows us to track every deal, every meeting, every contact … and ensures that I and others have the necessary overview." There was a degree of scepticism about the value of such an MIS; a scepticism that was fuelled by the inevitable early technical glitches. But Steve is adamant that it is – and will continue to prove – invaluable, infinitely superior to and more up to date and accurate than its predecessor. Furthermore it is a key tool of the top-level directors. What's good enough for them should be good enough for everyone else!

But the board's imprimatur is not only on the systems for growth. One of the most important key performance indicators (KPIs) in the boardroom is the extent to which BankCo has been successful in cross-selling its products and services. And this is no casual, internally generated back-of-the-envelope guesstimate. External auditors are employed to quantify BankCo's "share of wallet".

Finally BankCo has a method of reward that allows Steve and his counterparts to encourage their people to develop stronger and more profitable relationships with their clients. Of course – this is a bank, after all! – there are hard financial rewards; the revenues from new assignments go to the team that delivered the mandate. This is black income. But the mandate also creates an equivalent amount of what BankCo calls "white income". This is a central, all-company bonus pool and is allocated by Steve or his equivalent to all those who contributed to winning the mandate, irrespective of whether they were subsequently involved in its delivery; this "white income" then forms a major part of every individual's appraisal and bonuses.

"White income" is important – it allows Steve to reward a wider team for their contribution to success and lets individuals know that creating opportunities for others and supporting colleagues will be rewarded.

At the heart of BankCo's – and indeed all investment banks' – business model is client relationships: no relations mean no business. And Steve's role, like that of his counterparts in other divisions and all their teams, is to manage these client relations. And their ability to deliver is considerably enhanced by expensive and sophisticated management information systems, and by clear corporate signals: "white income" to reward the team for their contributions; share of each client's transactions being a key boardroom KPI; and perhaps above all through BankCo's determination to maintain and grow its business in tightly defined sectors.

Key lessons

> Knowing and publicizing your strengths and specific areas of expertise creates momentum internally and externally.

> Client knowledge is king.

> Rewards need both to recognize individual achievement and encourage cooperation.

3

What should happen – but doesn't

Anything as important, as valuable, as organic growth would surely be a company's top priority, correct? If everyone took organic growth as seriously as it deserved, organic growth would be organized, methodical, measured, systematic. It would be focused, planned and monitored constantly. Each team would have a day-to-day, dynamic and evolving plan to realize its growth potential based on a thorough analysis of the client's market opportunity, competitive activity and strategic objectives, which would be coloured by the adviser's in-depth understanding of the client organization, the personalities of the prime decision-makers and the state of the relationship. And above all this would be a hawk-like focus on opportunistic initiatives to deliver short-term competitive advantage to the client arising out of everyday news and market movements.

The process would not only be rigorously planned, but progress would be monitored constantly to ensure the plan is actually realized. It would be done *consciously and methodically.*

If you recognize the above you are very lucky and in a tiny minority. **Almost universally, it seems that the practice of achieving organic growth is haphazard, ad hoc, unfocused, rarely planned and invariably stop-start.**

In most professional service firms the primary focus is on the job that is currently most urgent – lurching from one project to the next. If there is a plan for growth it will sit in a dusty drawer, emerging briefly for a quick update at the Annual Review before settling back into its darkened space for the next 364 days.

Even when the plan is presented for its potential moment of glory and attention, it will be rushed through in a day's meeting that's also covering fifty other so-called priority clients, with a cast of thousands in a meeting room with no daylight and an audience that has lost its will to live by 11 a.m.!

Any organic growth opportunities normally result from ad hoc spurts of energy, or from side conversations with clients which catch the attention of the adviser – or from presenting one product after another, week in, week out, in the vain hope that if enough stuff is chucked at the client, something will stick. So organic growth becomes a hostage to fortune or a mission to bombard the client until he relents rather than the inevitable consequence of planning and initiative backed up by consistent energy. At best, this ad hoc approach results in the odd windfall project. You might strike lucky.

But the really outstanding performers in professional

service industries do not leave this prime driver of growth to chance. They do not engage in it when they have the time or go at it like some madman with a blunderbuss. Instead, they build the process into the core of their client offering.

Before moving on to what works and how to do it properly it is important to understand why this amateurish approach occurs and why a more professional, systematic and productive approach seems so difficult.

Issues that impede a properly organized approach

1   **There's no time.** In many professional services organizations, time is money. Literally. Every second spent working on a client's business is billable. We sell our time, so our time is valuable. Pick up the phone, the client is on the clock; send an email, the meter's ticking. From photocopying to financial forecasting, from basement to boardroom, everything we do and everywhere we go on the client's business is billable. Busy, busy, busy spells f-e-e-s.

You go to visit an investment bank, or a lawyer's office, or an advertising agency. Have a look round the office and you'll see two things: lots and lots of people typing and staring at computer screens; lots and lots of other people in vast meeting rooms having meetings. If you're a client, ask yourself: "Who's thinking, actually *thinking*, about *my* business?"

We sell our time, but we spend most of it in meetings or on email. And if I'm a client I want people to be thinking about my problems and issues.

The pressure to deliver, to react instantly to anything and everything via BlackBerry, via email, via mobile phone, reduces the quality of the thinking that is being done on the clients' behalf. And it could be argued that while clients are getting stuff done faster, the result might not be better or smarter. The fact that in many service sectors fewer and fewer people are shouldering more and more work means that most people working on client business have their hands full just finishing the job that's needed tomorrow, and are not adding value to the client's issues for next week, let alone next year.

We need to find ways of creating more time.

2 **New business is more glamorous**, attracting disproportionate rewards and talented people.

Obviously, every professional company needs to grow by winning new assignments – to refresh the client base, to bring new challenges to the firm's staff, to simply have something new to do. No firm can survive without some level of new business.

But why is it that a firm's heavy hitters are always available for a new client pitch, but somehow are less available to spend time on existing client development? And why is it that new business gets a disproportionate share of the glory? Why is it that organic growth is treated like Cinderella compared to the twin ugly stepsisters of new business and acquisition?

We know a company where they ring a bell every time they win a new client and immediately anyone who is around in the office drops everything they're doing and rushes to the main reception to hear the news of the client win and (normally) to grab a glass of champagne to help the winning team celebrate. Once everyone has gathered, the company CEO will make a short speech announcing the win and lauding the members of the team who have won the business. They are made to feel like heroes and, in addition to basking in the glory and acknowledging the plaudits of their colleagues, they usually receive a spot financial bonus in their next month's salary. Somehow, being part of that winning team makes the next promotion seem nearer, that new car more feasible and that extra responsibility more tangible. In this company, being part of a winning team that brings in new clients is the fastest route to being noticed and to career success.

At the same company, we heard the tale of a client executive who went in to see her board director. Bubbling with excitement, she told the director that her team had just been awarded an additional project from their aviation client, which would be worth an extra $35,000 in revenue. "At last you're doing your job, Cassie," snapped the director. End of conversation. No bell. No champagne. No gathering of the clans. No speeches. No promotion. Not even a "well done" or a "thank you".

But why do organizations exhibit such a contrast between the way they celebrate and honour new client wins and the way they disregard organic business development from existing clients? For every hero new business hunter, your organization has a huge need for really good farmers – winning new clients and then maximizing those relationships over the next five years often takes different types of people and different skills. Both types need recognizing, nurturing and rewarding.

And it's not just rewards and celebration which appear to be oriented towards new business. Ask people inside a professional service company whether there is a new business budget (yes), is someone senior responsible for new business (yes) and is there a properly resourced team for new business (yes)? Now ask the same three questions about organic growth – how long can you stand the silence?

We are *not* saying that new business should not have a budget and leadership, nor that it should not be rewarded. We are merely pointing out that organic growth is an unsung, unloved and therefore undernourished skill.

3   **There's a responsibility vacuum.** When we hear the phrase "business development is everyone's responsibility in this company", our blood runs cold. It may well be theoretically true that business development is "everyone's responsibility", but it also means that there is a real danger it becomes no one's responsibility. After all, if someone is failing to win more business they can shrug their shoulders and argue that it doesn't really matter because there's always someone else who is doing it. Isn't there?

This muddle is all too frequently evident in the way firms approach organic growth. The senior directors think it should be done by the middle managers, partly because they're at the coalface and so know more clients and more about the clients' business than they do, and partly because as senior directors they have more important matters to attend to: running the firm, promoting the industry ...

Meanwhile middle managers think it's the job of senior directors. Being at the coalface is hugely demanding; they are concentrating totally on delivering their projects on time, on budget and on specification. That is how they are judged and evaluated, and to think beyond the *now* is a waste of time and energy.

There's a similar muddle between relationship managers and technical experts. The former think the latter should be more client friendly and apply their expertise more consciously to client needs. The technical people think client relationships are simply not their responsibility. They provide the firm's skill base; it is for others to apply it.

4 **The fear factor.** The final barrier to organic growth is the fear factor. Fear that someone else in the organization will steal *my* income if I introduce them to *my* client. Fear that someone else in the organization will damage *my* relationship with *my* client because they may do an inferior job. This fear prevents cooperation, it discourages the discovery and sharing of opportunities. And fear shows. Clients can easily sense when a company is not working well internally, when individuals are more

worried about their position relative to their colleagues than the client.

The recruiter's tale

RecruitCo is the holding company for a young but now established recruitment consultancy with six key practice areas. They have 200 fee-earning consultants and operate primarily in the UK. They launched initially with one specialist practice and consciously decided that they needed to create a practice with its own identity in its employment sector. RecruitCo was simply an invisible holding company.

"We believed then that the only way we could break into this highly competitive area was to offer a real sense of expertise and focus; in effect saying to the market – "this is all we do'. When a few years later we launched our second practice, we followed a similar strategy. Partly because we wanted there to be clear water between the two practices but above all because we did not want this second practice to undermine the reputation of the first."

As other practices were launched, RecruitCo followed a similar pattern, creating sub-brands targeted at different market segments, each with their own strong individual reputation. They believed that this approach was more powerful than the alternative of creating a single "master brand" with generic descriptions of the practice area in which they operated.

This approach was enormously successful. Prospective candidates were clear about and attracted to a practice that really understood its job market; and their clients – mainly HR departments – recognized that they were able to attract higher-quality candidates within each sector by using this level of expertise and specialization.

Importantly, however, RecruitCo were clear that while outwardly they wished to present a family of separate specialist practices, internally they were determined to foster a common team culture. So while their employees worked in a practice area they were employed and rewarded centrally by RecruitCo.

"We were keen from day one that everyone who worked for us felt that they worked ultimately for the parent company. We wanted there to be a spirit of cooperation and helpfulness so that we could identify and pass on cross-practice opportunities as they arose."

But RecruitCo admits that, now established, they face some questions and challenges. First, they have reached a critical mass – they are able to compete at a corporate level with the far bigger players in the recruitment market. The early advantages of specialization are perhaps less obvious now that their reputation and scale have grown from the early start-up days. In particular, they believe that HR departments are now looking for synergies across different recruitment areas and that RecruitCo can and needs to adopt a more centrist approach. As one of the founding directors says: "We have had fantastic success building our business; about sixty per cent of our assignments come from just twenty per cent of our clients – we have worked very hard to maximize every opportunity to meet as many of the needs of our clients as possible. The question now is: how can we get more business from the other eighty per cent – and we suspect that we will need to rebalance the relative importance of our branded practice companies and that of the holding group. We are at a point where we are dealing with some of our clients as RecruitCo rather than as individual practice areas. After all, we deal mainly with a single client point – HR departments who are responsible for filling their company's vacancies across a wide number of sectors."

3 : What should happen – but doesn't

The second challenge is their rapid growth from small beginnings and few people to a bigger company and many people. It is far easier to create and maintain an internal culture of cooperation and mutual trust in a relatively small organization, but far harder in a bigger enterprise.

"In the past, everyone knew where they stood with one another. As we have grown there are more issues relating to whether and how we should reward people if they help another practice; or if they help cover for someone while they are away."

RecruitCo adopted a specific organic growth strategy. While their key clients are HR departments they felt that, in order to attract the best candidates and thus better meet the needs of their clients, they needed to create quite distinct and specialist practices. At the same time they wanted to ensure that the company worked as a company and did not splinter into competing and antagonistic units. This strategy has served them well. But today they face new challenges. Now established, they recognize that their model needs to adapt – with RecruitCo, previously a relatively silent presence, becoming more prominent – and they need to review how they can maintain and develop a strong internal team culture.

Key lessons

> (Most) clients want expertise and specialization; but this need not prevent internal cooperation.

> Success – and scale – may, in time, require different principles, systems and skills.

Part 1 summary

Taking organic growth seriously

Organic growth is hugely valuable: it is more profitable financially and creates stronger, better client relations. And it is the best new business tool ever invented! It is the ultimate proof of your abilities and talent.

There are many barriers to success: organic growth doesn't just happen. Recognizing and dealing with the barriers – lack of time or responsibility, the poor relation syndrome and sheer fear – are the first steps to the better future.

Getting your organization fit for organic growth

In this section we examine the four different types of organic growth you can pursue and look at some practical prerequisites to successful implementation. We cover how to grade your clients into high and low potential for growth, ways to organize your company and teams in pursuit of growth, creating growth action plans and recognizing and rewarding success. We also look at how best to overcome inertia and internal barriers from within your own organization. The section ends with a summary of the key actions to take in order to implement your new strategy.

4

If you don't believe you can help, don't try to sell

Proper professional client service does not mean trying to sell all your products to your client regardless of whether or not he needs them, or putting colleagues from other parts of your business in front of your client out of a desire to be fair to them or get your meeting quota up. If you are not acting out of the purest motives to help your client on the basis of some problem or genuine opportunity you have identified, then you will damage rather than enhance your relationship.

We know intuitively that this is the right way to behave, but put a little pressure on us to make this quarter's P&L target and we start putting our own interests ahead of the client's – doing damage to the relationship in the process.

> All too often we look at our clients' situation through the lens of our own offerings and our desire for another sale … building relationships does not mean "give us more work".
>
> *(Customer Service Market, Selling Professional Services, 18 March 2006)*

If the client always suspects that lurking behind every

one of your smiles is an order book waiting to be sprung on him, that everything he says will result in a fee proposal, that every contact is accompanied by a close, you will very soon become his *un*trusted adviser.

A colleague of ours spent over thirty years advising the P&G business at a variety of multinational advertising agencies. Wherever he went, his clients tracked him down and asked his new host agency to have him head up their business. Why? Because P&G value one thing in their advisers above all other things: honestly acting out of the best motives for the well-being of their organization. And once this client relationship supremo rose to the top heights of one of the world's biggest advertising holding companies, he evangelized his philosophy throughout the organization. His credo is simple: Act in the interests of the client's business first, the interests of the advisory firm second, and the interests of the individual third.

Thirty years working with a single client organization demonstrates a lot of love and a lot of dedication. But over and above everything, it demonstrates a remarkable level of trust between the client and this person. Trust based on a certainty, constantly reinforced by his every action, that his advice is offered with the best motive – the health of the client's business. "Stop selling, start helping!" as the management guru David Maister implores.

Another illustration of the need to believe that what you are recommending to your client is of genuine benefit to him and his organization comes from the head of a

US-based direct marketing consultancy. They call this guy "the Preacher" because of his tendency to wear black from head to foot, winter, spring, summer or fall. Now the Preacher had a client within the GE organization. And this client had used a new customer segmentation tool which had saved his division $175,000 on his direct marketing costs compared to the previous year. This client was very pleased with the Preacher and his company. Delighted by the savings his product had delivered to the GE client, the Preacher surmised that other colleagues of his client within the GE organization who also ran direct marketing programmes might be able to make similar significant savings by using his product.

The Preacher asked his client one day whether he'd be willing to host a meeting with a colleague from another division within GE so the product could be presented. The client declined on the basis that he was very busy at the time, but agreed to let the Preacher use his name by way of introduction. Armed with this, the name and direct-dial phone number of the target client, the Preacher made the call to try to set up a meeting. He got stonewalled by the client's personal assistant. So the next day, he tried again. And the next, and the next. In fact, he called every working day for seven months. Not once was he put through. He did, however – as you'd expect – get to know the client's personal assistant very well! So well, in fact, that he discovered that the boss was going to be taking a certain flight from New York to Chicago. The Preacher booked a ticket on the same flight. As there was free seating and he already knew what the client looked like, the Preacher walked up to the man and said:

"Excuse me, sir. My name is Tim. I do some work for a colleague of yours, Mr Stollenberg. We've managed to save his division $175,000 in the last year on his direct marketing activity with a product of ours which segments audiences more accurately than any other product on the market. I've been trying to get to see you for a few months because I believe we could help your division make similar savings. I'd like to sit here in the seat next to you. All I ask is five minutes of your time to tell you a little more. If you're not interested after that, I promise to be quiet for the rest of the journey. If you are interested, I'd love to find a way to help you save money."

Tim closed the deal on the plane. But that's not the point. The point is that you simply cannot sustain such a long-drawn-out campaign to engage with the client if you do not believe, truly believe, that you have a product or service that will make a real business difference to them. If you've been asked by a colleague to introduce them to your client, and you're doing it as a favour to your colleague rather than because you believe the client should hear what your colleague has to say, then if you get rebuffed at the first request you *might* have a second attempt. If you still get turned down, you'll give up – happy in the knowledge that you tried, relieved that you haven't pushed it too aggressively with your client.

Before you pick up the phone, send the email or ask for that meeting, ask yourself whether you are really convinced that you're asking for the meeting because you believe it will provide value to your client. If you don't believe, don't do it.

The urban planner's tale

TransPlanCo is a medium-sized (300 employees) consultancy specializing in urban design, transport, planning and infrastructure projects. Headquartered in London, and with three regional offices, they work internationally – particularly in the Middle and Far East. Their work is project based – they have no annuity clients, and while a few projects are long-term, their income visibility is measured in months, not years.

Graham has joined relatively recently as one of ten directors. When we began discussing the issue of organic growth, he said: "... we are constantly looking at the issue of repeat business and comparing it with new clients and new prospects ..." The reason for this internal discussion is that he and his fellow directors believe that the work they undertake must follow their Rule of Two. That is to say that any project must tick at least two of three boxes: a known client, a known location and a known specification.

"Given the variables of our world, of our clients and of local laws and regulations, our worst nightmare is to work with a new client, in an unfamiliar geography, on a mandate that we have never done before. There are just too many things that can go wrong, so we insist that we have at least two of these bases, and ideally all of them, covered."

So for TransPlanCo repeat business is a fundamental part of their business philosophy and culture. It is central to the way they work. Given this, it is perhaps surprising that their organic growth planning is relatively informal; other case histories will demonstrate more formal and rigorous systems and practices, but at TransPlanCo their approach is so integral to their culture that they believe that they can – and do – succeed without such systems.

But in reality there is method in their ways. While they have disciplines – areas of specialization – they have deliberately not adopted a rigid practice structure, each with its own P&L, which can lead to divisiveness and infighting. "It is an active part of our religion that we feed work wherever possible to others in the company." This behaviour is underpinned by policies such as bonuses being paid on an individual's overall contribution and not to their specific discipline. Stock option and purchase schemes also encourage a spirit of collaboration. And their religion is further enhanced by the relatively small size of the company; there are, for example, about one hundred in the main London office.

Graham states: "This is simply the way we do things round here. I don't know if it would work in a substantially larger organization – maybe not – but we believe that we have a long way to go before we hit that particular problem."

He also notes that he feels that the culture of their industry acts as a positive reinforcement of their own culture. Major urban and transport projects require an army of advisers and consultants. There is no single company that can undertake all the various aspects of these massive undertakings, and therefore there is a high degree of openness and cooperation between organizations. Architects need planners who need civil engineers who need contractors who need ... Graham believes that it is a "friendly industry with a strong dependency culture; I'm sure it helps foster the spirit of the way we work internally".

Finally, they understand the role of engaging with their clients outside the narrow constraints of the specific project. They are not lavish entertainers but they do have summer and Christmas parties. They see industry gatherings as an important means of maintaining contact with past and present clients. For instance, MIPIM, the world property market held annually in Cannes for real-estate professionals and investors, attracts 25,000-plus delegates from around the world. Many organizations see it as a great opportunity to meet and woo new prospects – and it is – but TransPlanCo view it completely differently. They use it as another opportunity to maintain their profile with their client base, to keep or get back in touch with clients.

But they do have two enemies that they have to guard against: forgetfulness and restlessness. Graham admits that sometimes they are poor at ensuring, as a project ends, that they organize their follow-up plan: how they are going to keep in touch, with whom, at what intervals, and so forth. As the project team breaks up and re-forms with other teams to become involved in new projects, this essential task can sometimes be overlooked.

TransPlanCo employ highly educated individuals – many with two degrees as well as serial professional qualifications. As is so often the case with bright people, they can become bored easily – they need and seek new challenges against which to pit themselves. The idea of repeating a project or working with the same client can cause frustration, and the directors have to ensure that people have a balance of the new and the familiar.

TransPlanCo is, frankly, an unusual case. Depending on your perspective, it is either backward in relation to organic growth – after all, it has few systems, policies or rewards that encourage the pursuit of organic growth – or it is among the most advanced – it simply doesn't need such systems because the ethos of getting more repeat business from existing clients is so deeply ingrained in the culture of the organization. Maybe the truth lies somewhere in between! But the power of a culture that regards organic growth as a given is clear.

Key lessons

> Working with existing clients can reduce corporate risk.

> Organic growth can be part of the corporate religion.

> Bright people need to be constantly remotivated.

5
Good practice, better practice

Most professional service companies employ a number of commonsense tactics to develop more business from their existing client base. They have keep-in-touch programmes ensuring that they are on their clients' – and prospects' – radar: daily email/text messages, conversations beyond the day-to-day. They will engage in wider networking activities: attending industry events and conferences or social occasions where they can widen their personal contacts. Most professional service companies undertake some publishing activity to promote their expertise and awareness.

These are good practices. But there are two problems. These activities are rarely undertaken consistently and rigorously. Everyone seems to agree that they are normally ad hoc, fall away when times are busy and could be done much better.

But the real problem is that however good your contact and network programmes, every other company is doing exactly the same thing. They too will be regularly in touch with their clients; they too will be networking. It is a necessary but ultimately zero-sum game.

The question, therefore, is not whether this is good practice (it is) but what can we do better?

The answer, we believe, lies in being more focused, devoting precious internal resources to fewer high-priority prospects.

1 Grade your clients

The first step in creating a more successful organic growth plan is to recognize that not all opportunities are equal. Not every client is necessarily of equal potential. You need to establish what the future revenue potential is of your clients: what your market share will be. This will create an initial priority list.

You need to grade your client base into A, B, C and D clients. This will help you determine not only on which clients to focus your resources and effort but also help you identify those clients that are sapping your company's energy and, even worse, diluting rather than enhancing your margin.

A clients are the key strategic clients on which the firm's energies must be deployed most effectively in pursuit of organic growth. Your company will have a very strong relationship with these clients, and your client contacts will be strong advocates for your firm within their organization and in the wider business community. You will be doing your best work already for these clients and you will have identified opportunities to help them reach their key business objectives (which you will know and understand) or avoid dangers they may not have foreseen, as well as highlighting areas of their operation where they currently have no representation in your firm's area of expertise or have a vulnerable relationship with one of your competitors. A-list clients will be dynamos within their own market sectors and operate within markets that are growing rapidly. Therefore they represent very high growth potential. They may be large or small enterprises.

B clients will be client companies with whom you enjoy very good solid relationships and where there is a good level of activity – but not as dynamic and fast growing as with A clients. They may be slower moving and less immediately responsive to initiatives you present and their decision-making processes will probably take longer. But they will be the bedrock of your client revenue base and as such it is essential not just that you invest time and resources in them but that you are seen to do so actively.

C clients have a service-and-maintain status. You may well have a good relationship, but they will never have the business growth and revenue potential of A and B clients. They are "nice to have" clients to whom you will continue to provide solid professional service but in whom you will not invest ahead of revenue in order to grow the business – because it will not grow at a rate commensurate with the time investment required.

D clients should probably be culled from your client list.

They will be margin dilutive, they will sap the energy of the team that has to service them, they will quibble over all invoices and they will never be satisfied. They will keep you under constant threat of review or may fire you before you get the chance to fire them. But if you do fire them, you will see morale rise in your organization very rapidly as your team members walk taller knowing that the company they work for stands up for itself. It is rumoured that McKinsey cull the bottom 10% of their client base every year. And it doesn't seem to have done them much harm ...

The Three Fs

There is another way of evaluating which clients to focus on: we call it the three Fs.

The idea is that any client that has any two of the three is probably worthy of investment.

> F Fortune (a big fee earner with lots of revenue potential).

> F Fame (a high-profile client with a level of credibility in excess of its fee potential).

> F Fun (a client with whom your staff enjoy working and who feels the same way about you).

2 Reality check

But beyond revenue potential there are some other simple reality-check criteria. The three most important are:

Is your current relationship secure; and what is your client satisfaction score?

You must have a robust relationship in order to successfully seek more work – we believe a relationship score of 8/10 is the minimum required; much less than this would suggest that there may be problems closer to home which need fixing first. And we believe that it is vital to have objective feedback channelled through independent relationship auditors. If you're marking your own homework, you're heading for trouble.

If you are seeking to oust a competitor, is this realistic? You may believe (and perhaps rightly so) that your company can do a job that is as good if not better than your rival's. But the question is whether the client believes that your potential performance is enough to displace a relationship that may be long standing, run deep or be immovable for other reasons.

Finally, there is an honesty box question – **is the new service(s) or product(s) that you wish to offer really up to standard?** Time and time again, when we are advising our own clients we find they often have a somewhat over-optimistic approach to their own capabilities. They claim to be able to do far more than seems humanly possible. The real question is what does the firm do *extremely* well, not merely what can it do or what has it done in the dim and distant past?

3 The firm needs to involve the widest team, with clear roles

Organic growth cannot be one person's responsibility; it is too important to be managed and delivered by a single person.

Partners need to be involved. They have the client contacts; they have the experience of the business; they have expertise and authority. And they must lead internally – if senior partners are not in tune with and supportive of organic growth, why should anyone else take it seriously?

Middle managers are at the daily coalface and therefore should know the client and their issues more deeply. They will also be aware of some of the personal or political factors that need to be considered. And they are important because if they don't deliver today then future opportunities for more business are severely diminished.

Finally, technical experts and even back-room or support staff should be included in some or all of the planning or implementation. They need to know what's going on in order to play their part, but can also provide invaluable ideas and insights. When we run Organic Growth Workshops we always want as many of the team present as possible. We are constantly amazed by the contribution, wisdom and insight offered by those behind the scenes.

4 Put resources behind your efforts

The next step is to create a budget of resources. But above all, make allowance for that most precious commodity of all – time.

A financial budget can be easily determined. If you have

clear targets with a known monetary value you can estimate an investment budget. If you spend x dollars pitching y dollars' worth of new business, you should apply the same formula to an organic growth opportunity. In reality the financial investment is likely to be far less; you know a considerable amount already and costs are likely to be disproportionately lower.

While creating more time may seem impossible, if you add up all the faffing-around time that happens in the office – the impromptu gossip meetings around the water cooler, the just-popped-in-for-a-chat meetings five times a day, the constant compulsion to read and reply to email as it arrives rather than in preordained time slots dedicated to managing correspondence – you could liberate at least 10% extra time, which could be used to invest in thinking about a client's issues.

We'll talk about how to organize that time to best effect, where to focus the effort and what to talk about in more detail later, but in a nutshell, convert the unprofitable faffing-around time into potentially lucrative investment time thinking about and discussing your client's issues (*not* the day-to-day work you're already doing for them). And don't bill the client for the time because this is an investment you're making in yourselves as well as in the client. (Incidentally, if the client's procurement people come knocking, the ability to demonstrate thinking-time investment in the client's business shows hidden value that can be used as evidence of your company's commitment to the client.)

Recommendation: set aside 5% of your week to think about the client's business *in the round.* In an average working week of 40 hours, a 5% investment will give you two hours' clear thinking time with your team (or on your own) on your A and B clients' issues. Think what miracles of opportunity you could unearth that will lead to potentially profitable conversations with the client if you did this every week. Two hours a week is eighty hours a year in a forty-working-week year – or ten working days. If you multiply the cost of that at your full billable rates and evaluate it against the return you get in new incremental income as a result, we'd posit you'll have a very respectable ROI.

And by the way, if you think it is unrealistic to free up ten working days in your already overburdened schedule, just remember that somehow people manage to squeeze at least ten days from somewhere to work on a new business pitch and devote time to thinking about a complete stranger's business issues!

5 Create a plan of action

Having prioritized your clients, assembled a team and created a budget of time – and maybe other resources – you can more confidently create a plan of action. Every plan should have **two key elements: who and why.**

You need a clear map of the client's organization – who you know, who you need to get to know, who reports to whom, who influences whom, who controls the budgets, who makes executive decisions. Your existing knowledge and contacts can begin the process; research and that old-fashioned concept of asking will provide the rest.

The second element is two questions that you need to keep constantly at the back of your mind as you develop and implement an organic growth programme. Why should the client company give us more business – what are the benefits to them? And why should this person – or department – give us more business? What's in it for them (particularly if they have to surrender a relationship with another supplier to work with you)? **The question is: what's in it for our client, NOT what's in it for us?**

6 Implement the plan

A plan needs to be implemented. There is every reason and incentive to embed the plan in the rhythms of the daily work you do; it should be a regular item at internal status meetings, and be reviewed at least quarterly. Above all it must not become that tired and dusty once-a-year document that can never provide the necessary momentum.

7 Recognize and reward

Remember Cassie, our hapless executive whose efforts in winning an extra assignment from her aviation client went unrecognized and unrewarded, and who consequently felt that her role was severely undervalued? Everyone needs recognition, and if the new business hunters get their moment in the spotlight, so too should heroic farmers.

Next time someone comes into your office with news of a new project from an existing client, ring your company bell! Break out a bottle or two and make that person and the team feel that they just did something really significant. Because they did.

The lawyer's tale

Lucinda is not a lawyer but holds one of the most important roles in her firm, LawCo, a large multinational legal practice. She does not directly generate revenue but is instrumental in helping others earn their fee income. She is an unbillable in a world where the billable is king.

Lucinda works for the London office of LawCo, which has the classic practice structure of most legal companies and about a hundred partners. Her role is to lead the business development team, and she was hired specifically to implement a programme of organic growth – developing more assignments from LawCo's existing client base.

As one of the senior partners said: "We can continue to act as a group of semi-independent fiefdoms and we will probably be reasonably successful. But we will not realize the full potential of the firm as a whole until and unless we operate as one team working for our clients on a broader spectrum of their challenges."

Lucinda had worked in a number of other professional service companies before joining LawCo, and is clear about the challenges facing not only her company but others in implementing such a vision. These include:

> **Lack of focus**: with over a thousand clients, the hundred-plus partners cannot possibly manage their portfolio in any meaningful way.

> **Short-termism**: business development is about long-term, deep client relationships; too many professional service organizations look to the short term and today's revenues, profits and bonuses.

> **The cult of the brochure**: too many think another brochure is the zenith of marketing; it is activity, yes, but activity that is an inadequate substitute for proper marketing.

> **Billable rules, OK**: the tyranny of the billable system is that it requires the individual to maximize his or her client hours. It works against anything that is not directly attributable to a project fee.

> **Lack of time**: there is no successful company that has enough time. Individuals, and particularly those in demand, can and do work 24/7. Even where business development is on the agenda it gets done at weekends – meaning it doesn't get done!

Overall, while business development is generally recognized as a good thing, the reality is that it proves nearly impossible to deliver. As Lucinda said: "Business development [in professional service organizations] is almost universally acknowledged as a key to future growth. The accountants got there ten years ago and the lawyers are catching up fast. It's one thing to accept the principle, but it is incredibly difficult to implement."

With the support of the senior partners, Lucinda created a strategic and operational plan to address these issues. A key element was to focus on a small number of A-client (Level 1) prospects. Lucinda asked us to guess how many, and bearing in mind that LawCo has over a thousand clients we answered in the 100–200 range. The actual number is thirty. Just 3% of their client base is regarded as Level 1 Prospects. They were selected not only on the basis of current and future revenue potential but on their strategic importance to LawCo.

A similar exercise revealed a further seventy clients who were designated as Level 2 prospects. LawCo looked at business sectors where they wished to make inroads or deepen their penetration. And they chose a company within each sector which they felt would be an exemplary target for that sector.

Lucinda rightly emphasizes that this hierarchy of Level 1 and 2 prospects does not mean that the service received by these prospects is superior to that received by others. "The point of this exercise was not to rebalance the efforts and expertise of the firm in our professional capacity; it is simply to reprioritize where and how we spend our own development resources."

This prioritization process is simple to describe, but was far less easy to agree internally, with considerable debate and not a little dissent. But having got to this point eventually, the next element was to agree the implementation plan. Two partners were designated as Client Development Leaders (CDLs) for each of the thirty Level 1 prospects; in addition, about ten other partners drawn from the various practices were assigned to each pair of CDLs to support their endeavours.

Lucinda chairs a monthly meeting of this team of twelve with a brutally simple agenda;

1 **Progress review**: are we achieving our growth objectives?

2 **Relationship review**: who has met whom with what outcomes?

3 **The future**: who is doing what within three time frames – thirty, sixty and ninety days?

And at least every six months, a senior partner attends these monthly meetings. (The seventy Level 2 prospects were similarly resourced but with a smaller team of just two partners.)

The strategy of intense focus on a few key prospects and the commitment of a dedicated cross-discipline team to realize the opportunities may seem obvious. But in a practice-based company such as LawCo (or an accountant or a bank or a consultancy …) it is easy to underestimate these cultural and practical barriers to success.

Many partners in many professional service organizations are totally committed to their calling, their vocation. They see business development as a lower-order skill, well beneath their radar and even dignity. Indeed, many partners are more committed to their practice than the firm as a whole, which is merely a place where they pursue their higher-order vocation. And many are fiercely protective of their client relationships, proud of their own client intimacy and fearful that others will either jeopardize or steal what they regard as their lunch. Thus to get a partnership to be involved in business development, to place the interests of the firm above those of their own practice and to share their clients with others, is a simply massive achievement.

Lucinda is clear about the four ingredients that helped transform LawCo.

1 **Leadership**: the senior partners set the strategy, the agenda and actively participated in the programme. Lucinda describes this as aggressive leadership. Their leadership also included accepting – in some cases encouraging – the departure of a small number of partners who were uncomfortable with the new world.

2 **The CDL team structure**: the existence of the thirty CDL teams sent out a powerful message of intent to the partners and the whole of LawCo: this is for real. The two CDLs on

each team were chosen because of their ability to think and act beyond the constraints of the practice culture. They were role models for others throughout LawCo. And the team structure itself created important interdependencies; it broke down practice barriers and created new personal connections – on average, a partner would participate in three CDL teams.

3 **Rewards**: the eat-what-you-kill fee culture is powerfully ingrained but rewards and evaluation are changing. Partners are being assessed not only on their fee-earning abilities, but on their wider contribution. Time spent on client development is accounted for as if it were client-billable hours. CDL team leaders are recognized as *primus inter pares*.

4 **Resources**: Lucinda has a significant team working for her. They include commercially aware business managers, database and IT experts, a knowledge and Web group, analysts and communication professionals. Their task is to ensure that the necessary knowledge, insights and training are readily available to the partners. "We do the grunt work; they do the glory!"

The results of this business development programme are truly impressive. Confidentiality prevents detailed disclosure, but LawCo is one of the fastest-growing organizations not only in its own network, but in the London market.

Perhaps the most telling symbol of success is Lucinda's own story. As mentioned, she has worked in other professional service organizations. She is passionate and articulate about her work, but she had been frustrated at her previous employers. She – and they – knew what to do, but were unable to make it happen. At LawCo she has found an organization that knows not only what to do but how to do it, and how to do it consistently.

Key lessons

> Leadership from and by the top makes a huge difference.

> Focus on a few key clients.

> Ensure the internal organization and rewards structure reflects the mission.

> Organic growth isn't free; it needs serious resources!

6
The four different types of organic growth

Any organic growth strategy will fall into one of four broad areas which will be defined by two axes: whether or not you already work with the client, and whether or not the service(s) you are offering is already used by the client.

We have identified the most common challenges that will face any organic growth plan depending on its position within this matrix.

		Client	
		existing	new
Service	existing	A	C
	new	B	D

A Selling an existing product or service to an existing client
(you already do XYZ for client ABC – how can you do more XYZ more often?)

This is arguably the easiest source of incremental assignments and income. The client knows you and your work so you are building on solid foundations.

The key priorities are:

> be alert and organized so every opportunity is taken;

> know and work with the client's planning and budgetary cycles;

> constantly remind them of your past and current successes with them;

> take the initiative by seeking improvements in process or on costs.

The major barrier to success in this area is boredom. Professional service companies employ highly educated, smart and intellectually restless individuals for whom the idea of doing the same thing over and over again is anathema. They thrive on change, they need the stimulus of the new.

One company ran enormously successful brainstorm workshops with and for their clients. These workshops created strong team bonds between client and company, were highly stimulating and enjoyable and, above all, created new ideas and initiatives which became the source of future projects and income. But the company had stopped doing them.

The reason was that they were simply bored after doing a few of these sessions and so they had fallen by the wayside. The solution was simplicity itself: run the workshops but use people who did not work on that client's business. This meant that different client teams created workshops for others' clients, which created the necessary buzz of adrenalin and had a further benefit in helping minimize a client silo mentality.

B Selling a new service to an existing client (you wish to sell a new service to client ABC for whom you already do XYZ).

There will be two problems to overcome. The first is that your client has pigeonholed you as doing only XYZ. He is unwilling to see you as capable of doing RST. Indeed, the client may see your approach as undermining your expertise in the area in which they hired you in the first place. You will have to work hard to overcome this prejudice in order to demonstrate your capabilities in this new area:

> running seminars to demonstrate your expertise;

> attending or speaking at industry events;

> introducing your partners in this practice area;

> reassuring clients that performance will not be undermined by additional work.

The second problem is that you may get this new RST work only if you can replace an existing competitive supplier. There are two key questions that must be addressed:

> Is there an incumbent? And if so, is it realistic to supplant them or are they so entrenched as to be immovable?

> What are the benefits to the company and to the individual client(s) of assigning you new and additional work?

C Selling an existing service to another client

(you currently do XYZ for client ABC; you wish to do XYZ for another client in a different department or division).

Here the support and endorsement of your existing client is important, specifically in helping you gain access to and a hearing from the new client(s). This is the key priority – to develop a relationship with the new prospect – and it should be approached as one would approach a new business pitch.

Another issue you need to consider is that your existing client may become jealous. He may be worrying that the relationship he has with you may be diluted, that his work from you will suffer, that he may be displaced in your company's priorities. Performance with your existing client needs to be immaculate, and you may have to consider adding to the team so that each client gets their own dedicated resources.

D Selling a new service to a new client
(you work with the corporation but believe there is an opportunity to go way beyond your current remit and client).

This is the hardest opportunity to crack. It is, in reality, a new business pitch and should be planned as such.

The PR's tale

PRCo is a public relations company employing about eighty people. Its principal clients are consumer-facing organizations with mass audiences whom PRCo reaches via traditional mainstream media channels, although with an increasing emphasis on digital channels. It does not offer some of the more specialist PR services such as investor relations, healthcare or public affairs/lobbying.

John has no doubts that "... organic growth is cheaper and far less disruptive than new-business pitching. After all, a pitch involves lots of resources and particularly senior people, is non-billable and you've only got, if you're lucky, a one-in-four chance of winning!"

He was, however, equally quick to point out the challenges of growing organically. First, clients tend to categorize and to pigeonhole. The initial assignment you win defines how the client sees you into the future. It is difficult to break out of this mindset.

"If you hire a decorator, you might allow them to do other minor repairs in the house. But if he says that he can replace the central heating system or build an extension you feel less comfortable: is a decorator really able to move into a whole new activity? What's more, you begin to doubt if he is as capable a decorator as you first thought."

Second, in a mature and established market such as PR, clients are well aware of the strengths and weaknesses of firms in different sectors; who are the players in public affairs, who in healthcare, who in investor relations. Furthermore, individuals or departments who control the budgets for these areas and make decisions about which agencies to employ are normally different people; the investor relations team is separate from the consumer PR team.

PRCo took two decisions about how they could grow their business organically. They decided that they would stick to their core business: consumer PR. They felt that the barriers to expanding their offer into other sectors were too great to warrant the necessary investment and exposure to risk. They decided that they could grow by doing more of the same – expanding their assignments by working well and successfully with their established clients.

But they did take advantage of smaller incremental opportunities if they related to their core expertise.

"For example, our clients might need some consumer research, or design work or media training ... These were all projects that we could undertake because they came off the back of the work we were doing and within an existing relationship. Our clients trusted us to do this work because we were delivering on our core business. But we never went out into the marketplace to sell ourselves independently as a fully fledged research company or a design studio or whatever. We knew our limits but stretched those limits as far as we realistically could."

This is a tale of realism and self-awareness. Yes, there were opportunities to grow and PRCo could have tried to become a bigger entity offering more and more services outside its original specialization of consumer PR. But the company believed that this would be impossibly difficult. Instead they focused on the sector and clients with whom they had an established and successful reputation.

Key lessons

> Be selective about your skills. Less can be more.

> Incremental opportunities may be small but disproportionately valuable.

7

Overcoming the internal barriers to organic growth

There are many barriers to be overcome in pursuit of better organic growth. Not least of these are the barriers you will encounter from within your own company. People are often very territorial about their client relationships – and this is quite right and proper (and also understandable) if it is born out of a motivation to do right by the client rather than to protect an individual's own P&L. If you are determined to prevail in this pursuit, however, you had better be prepared to meet any resistance fully armed. Below are the seven most common objections made against taking the initiative with the client:

1 We've tried all this before – the client's not interested.

2 We've had the client only a little while – we don't want to seem pushy.

3 We should just focus on the job at hand.

4 The client's perfectly happy with their existing adviser in the area we think is an opportunity.

5 I'm too busy.

6 The client is too busy.

7 I don't want to damage my relationship with the client if someone else screws up on delivery.

To help you overcome these barriers, here are some responses to these common objections:

1 We've tried all this before – the client's not interested

> Don't accept this excuse at face value. What did happen last time? What lessons can we learn? Has the situation (or the people) changed?

> Befriend the client in a disinterested way; look for opportunities to help selflessly; put together a new offer with an added dimension in combination with another part of your business the client values, or with another of the client's suppliers or divisions.

> Escalate up the client company/your firm's hierarchy

> Keep helping and something good will happen. We call it psychic income – one day you'll be able to cash in the goodwill you bank with the client.

2 We've had the client only a little while – we don't want to seem pushy

> Early in the relationship is when you must exhibit hunger and commitment. There's no need to be pushy

but laying down a marker showing that you want this to be a mutually growing and developing relationship must be a good move.

> *Now* is the only time this will be easy (before you get pigeonholed).

In a new relationship you have every right to ask questions, show an appetite for knowledge and understanding and exhibit enthusiasm. You also have the benefit of the doubt.

Taking the initiative demonstrates that you have been thinking about the client's business (what every client wants from his advisers, surely?).

There really are only three opportunities to get more work from clients: at the beginning of the particular job at hand (when other unforeseen needs might crop up), in the middle of the job (when levels of excitement are high) or at the end of the job (which we think is the worst time to ask for more business). We cover this in more detail later on, in Chapter 17. But asking early is a great way to make your mark.

3 We should just focus on the job at hand

> The current job and its delivery are indeed determinants of future opportunities; but they are not the *only* determinants. The quality of the relationship and its value to the client should be bigger than the job in hand.

> If you get a new project, more resources can be

allocated so the existing project is never compromised.

> Find a benefit for the client (why should they give you more business?). This might be the financial and time advantage the client gains by not having to hunt constantly for the best particular firm for every particular need – a classic outsourcing/integrating proposition.

4 The client is perfectly happy with their existing adviser

> Can you match or better your competitor's strengths? Can you identify weaknesses that you might use? In essence, is this a real objection?

> If it is, be a helpful and disinterested friend.

Be understanding. Acknowledge that the competition are competent. Be honest: we really want to do more business with you. Ask whether the client will allow you to present proposals with no obligation to them. Sell interesting proposals, benchmark their current supplier. Get a date on which to present: the client is, after all, just being responsible by seeing what else is available on the market.

> If it isn't a real objection, it's just a brush-off! Behave as above and keep going.

5 I'm too busy

> If you've identified this client as a key growth target, get a senior champion within your firm.

> Put this client on your status report.

> Allocate 5% of your weekly time to thinking about this client.

> Are you really too busy? Is the urgent always driving out the important?

6 The client is too busy

> Clients are never too busy to look at good ideas, better results and enhanced value. If your proposal is any of these, the client will make time. And you'll know whether you've scored a direct hit because the client will stay engaged and run late for his next meeting. So you must allow an extra thirty minutes before and after the official client meeting, (a) in case the client wants to keep talking, and (b) because you'll often pick up useful intelligence or bump into someone else who might need help.

7 I don't want to damage my good relationship with the client if someone else screws up on delivery

> Only introduce people you trust. If you're the one asking for the introduction, it's beholden on you to take your sponsor through your proposal, take their guidance, and rehearse both your presentation and your answers to any questions you or your sponsor anticipate that the client will ask. In short, this is a pitch, so treat it like one and treat your colleague's precious relationship with the client with great

respect. If you're the one making the introduction, insist on a rehearsal so you know what's going to be presented. No rehearsal, no meeting!

> Get senior air cover at your company.

> Think of the upside if it goes brilliantly!

The designer's tale

BrandCo is an international corporate identity company. A new management team arrived to find a struggling company: revenues falling, reputation weakening and new business faltering.

A symptom of the state of the company was a telephone conversation with a client who asked if BrandCo had any information on a particular industry sector. "No; but we could do some work and research to answer your question." "But," replied the client, "I thought you only did work which interested you rather than being bespoke to our needs?"

As the MD said: "This was terrifying. It was as if we had become an academic organization, a benign institute more interested in our own issues than those of our clients."

They regarded winning back the confidence of their existing clients as a major objective. It was, in their words, the key to recovery. They knew that their first priority was to restore and rebuild existing client relationships. Only then could they engage confidently with other prospects.

They embarked on a three-pronged strategy.

Restructuring: they replaced an unwieldy executive board populated with lifers and people with obscure and irrelevant responsibilities with a tight three-person executive – CEO, COO, CFO.

They also abandoned the multi-practice structure. Like many service companies, BrandCo company had been organized into separate practices, each with their own P&L account, which in turn determined the bonuses of the team. But they had become secretive empires and on occasion competitive with one another. There were examples of one practice withholding client information or opportunities from another, even if they were more suited to a project, because the incumbent practice was frightened that they would lose work or the client relationship. The net result was poor client service, and poor delivery as practices sought to protect their income and relationships.

Refocusing: the new management made the key decision that there needed to be a real sense of purpose within the company and that this required some tough decisions about people and clients. Within a few weeks there had been a significant redundancy programme based on the principle of making one major push in this area rather than a continuing series of smaller cuts over time. The company also terminated its relationship with some clients, notably those who offered limited future potential or were a drain on resources and profit.

Leading from the front: the new CEO and COO made it their mission to see and be seen, to meet with clients regularly and to get their own hands dirty by becoming intimately involved in as many projects as possible. They were determined to show their people and their clients that the company could do great work and create valuable partnerships. As they commented: "You have to do three things – build relationships, deliver and then over-deliver and thus build a relationship that is based on trust."

This high-level engagement was complemented by a recruitment programme, hiring "better, conspicuously smarter people" to ensure that the work and delivery were of the highest standards.

The results have been dramatic – a company now delivering record profits, a growing client base and a reputation that is now restored to its former glory. The success of the new team has been recognized through significant promotions, and the company attracts and retains a far better calibre of employee.

They have even restored the practice structure, but with one significant difference. Whereas previously rewards were based on a practice's own P&L, rewards are now allocated on the basis of overall client revenues irrespective of which practice does the work. A growing client income means a bigger pot for everyone.

There are many lessons within this case study, among them the need to focus on hiring, retaining and motivating outstanding people, providing them with a structure that is cohesive not divisive, and taking some tough decisions early.

But the overarching lesson is that to grow existing client revenues the top management have to get involved. In the case of BrandCo, this meant rolling up their sleeves and actually doing the work – a clear demonstration to clients and employees alike that they meant business and that their standards were to be the target and ambition of the whole company.

Key lessons

> **Getting more business from existing clients is the best new business credential.**

> **Existing leadership, structures and people may need major surgery to achieve the objective.**

> **Silo mentalities must be eradicated.**

8

Setting your organization up for effective cross-selling

Cross-selling each other's expertise to a client is, in the words of the Bard, "a consummation devoutly to be wished". But in practice, as we have shown, it is phenomenally difficult to achieve. There are many barriers to be overcome. But there are also many positive moves that can be made to set up the conditions inside your company which make successful cross-selling more likely to happen.

The question is, how do you do it?

Be in a state of readiness when opportunities arise

Successful cross-selling requires a change in the way professional service companies traditionally operate and behave. It requires departments and people to work together in new ways in order to unlock new revenues organized around client need rather than around the company's silos of specialist skills. And nothing galvanizes this process faster than client demand. As the

CEO of a global advertising agency group once commented: "Thank God for clients. We'd never put in place all these new systems and create these new ways of working if we were left to our own devices!"

Or, as Newton put it in his First Law of Motion: "Unless acted upon by a net force, a body at rest stays at rest, and a moving body continues moving at the same speed in the same straight line."

If you want to create real, proper momentum behind a drive to cross-sell, you need a client sponsor to make it urgent. In short, you need "a burning platform". Otherwise it remains a goal, a nice-to-have rather than a must-have.

But if you do not have a clear and present need from a client, there are a few positive actions you can take in order to prepare for when there is a client need. If you take these actions, you will be in a state of readiness to take quicker and better advantage of opportunities when they arise.

You can promote awareness and understanding between the different parts of your organization, and you can encourage a greater degree of personal familiarity between the people who will have to collaborate when the time comes.

Awareness and understanding

There is often a lack of understanding that exists within professional service companies between different silos. Often this manifests itself in some very fundamental ways:

> different ways of working;

> different knowledge management systems;

> ignorance of each other's client base (not just across geographic borders but also within different disciplines within the same building);

> different presentational styles, format and fonts;

> different timescales of payback on effort.

"Ignorance" will be costing your company money

It will be costing you in terms of the duplication of effort, in terms of reinventing processes every time each division goes to visit a client, and in terms of paying for the same thing twice or more. And it will be costing you in terms of corporate reputation if your clients spot that your left hand and your right hand don't seem to know what the other is doing. Clients like to know that their suppliers communicate within their organizations to ensure they aren't inconsistent in their advice and that information passed on from the client is transmitted efficiently.

If your people don't know *of* each other, let alone actually *know* each other, then this ignorance will be costing your organization an untold but very large sum of potential revenue. Just by making your people aware of the services and specialist areas in which your organization can help clients, you will go a long way to opening the doors to cross-selling opportunity. Education works!

Take the time to educate your people on the company's capabilities. Put them in learning workshops together (they might forge good and useful friendships) and produce a handy, hard-copy (as well as electronic) *Rough Guide* to each of your company's services so they can reference it easily. And write the guide in language that's entertaining as well as informative – that way people will remember it. If it's written in jargon-laden gibberish and as dull as ditchwater, make each division write their entry again. You want people to *use* the information the next time their client says, "Do you have any expertise within your organization on XYZ?" and to give a well-informed, positive answer. You do not want them to sound ignorant, hesitant or, worst of all, say to the client that this isn't an area your firm is proficient in when, in reality, it is.

When each of your divisions presents its capabilities to the other divisions, ensure that they make it interesting and compelling. If you sit people in a room and they have to listen to someone drone on and on about one of the other division's capabilities, the audience may be physically present, but their attention will be elsewhere. Write the presentation from *the audience's* point of view: what do *they* want to know? What questions might they have? What concerns are worrying them? What might their clients find useful? Make the effort to inform, educate *and entertain*, and you'll go a long way to knocking over the awareness barrier and thus to addressing the issue of general ignorance that is costing the company millions.

Once you start this programme, keep it going

People move jobs. Up to a third of staff may move out of the company in any given year (taking all that knowledge, expertise and client goodwill with them). So maintaining awareness levels across your company at a proper level will require constant attention. It's a bit like painting the Forth Bridge: the moment you think you've finished painting it, you have to start all over again at the beginning. But it's worth the effort.

Invest in the right skills training

You will also need to invest in training. Training your people in specialized technical knowledge will need to be complemented by investment in skills that will *really* unlock incremental client revenue: learning how to present well, learning how to structure a written proposal so it is both logical and compelling, learning about different types of people and how best to communicate with them, learning how to create rapport and how to manage client relationships. In most professional service organizations these skills are often referred to as **"soft"** skills. Believe us, there is nothing soft about being able to persuade brilliantly, or being able to motivate a team, or being able to listen really attentively. These are without doubt the **hardest** and most profitable skills you can invest in for your people. They are what turns all that technical knowledge into urgent, compelling arguments which make clients want to take action.

Make your people *aware* of each other's skills and help them *understand* why those skills are valuable to clients.

Familiarity

In business, that old saying "familiarity breeds contempt" doesn't hold. In business, *familiarity breeds favourability* – not only between client and adviser, but, more crucially for cross-selling purposes, between different parts of your own organization. The simple truth is that we respond better and quicker to people we know, like, respect and care about. If the people in your different silos are strangers to each other, forget trying to cross-sell. You are wasting your time and energy.

How many times are teams brought together to make a cross-specialist presentation to a client when the individual members of that group have never met personally, have no track record of working together, do not know anything about each other, do not even know what each other look like? Far too often, the team isn't a team at all. It's just a group of specialists flung together at the last minute, who are underprepared, under-rehearsed and who will jet in for the meeting only to jet out again straight after it. And these teams are expected to look and behave like a coherent, unified unit brought together to make 1 + 1 = 3 for the client they are supposedly helping.

Quick team building

If you cannot use a team whose members are familiar
with each other, and which has worked together in the
past, then at least insist that the team meets regularly by
phone or video conference as you prepare your material
for the client presentation. And insist that the team gets
together twenty-four hours ahead of the client meeting.
Get everyone into the room together. Don't just launch
into the business agenda – take a little time out to get
everyone introduced. And don't use the creeping death
technique whereby everyone, in turn, goes round the
table introducing themselves! There's nothing duller
than twenty people going through their name, rank and
serial number in formal sequential order.

Instead, so that you build knowledge and history
between the team members really fast, get them to pair
up and spend two minutes finding out about each other:
something they feel passionate about, where they go on
holiday, what their proudest achievement is, a little-
known and unusual fact about each person. Then get
each person to introduce the individual they've just
spent two minutes interrogating. Bingo – instant energy
and instant history being built before your eyes.

Only once you've done all this should you proceed to
discussing the actual work. Then, at the end of the
session, *don't* let everyone rush back to their BlackBerries.
Insist that the whole team goes out and has a meal and
some drinks together. An hour and a half round the
dinner table is a better investment than a hundred
conference calls or a million emails.

When you turn up at the client's office the next day, you'll look, act and come over as a better, more unified team. You will appear a like-minded team of people working together to solve the problem, not a bunch of hired guns in it for themselves. Teams win the hearts and minds of clients.

Debrief

After the presentation, have a debrief. Resist the temptation to rush to the airport and scatter to the four winds. A debrief is essential because it helps the team to learn and improve and also to decide what needs to happen next.

It is no surprise that the Royal Air Force crack aeronautical display team, the Red Arrows, train for six months together. They get to know each other very well. They fly through the same aerobatic manoeuvres five times a day, every day for six months, in order to perfect the split-second timing that thrills crowds all over the United Kingdom every summer.

But this isn't what produces the spectacular end result.

What makes the difference, what makes the Red Arrows world class, is the debrief they go through after each and every training flight. In the debrief the flight team deconstruct every flight manoeuvre, go over every imperfect move, analyse the technical performance.

The Red Arrows get a lot of repeat business. They must be doing something right.

Part 2 summary

Getting your organization fit for organic growth

Be selective and focused: concentrate and dominate. Zero in on A and B client opportunities which are resourced sufficiently in terms of time, people and money rather than spreading your efforts too thinly out of well-intentioned but ultimately ineffectual ambitions.

Create a budget: certainly of time (5%) and ideally of money required to fund an initiative or research project – to think about and better understand the client's business.

Work as a team: it's unlikely that any one person can identify and secure a growth opportunity. The whole team, including the most senior people, have to be engaged. They all have a role to play.

Have a plan: too often so-called client plans are merely a vision or a dream of success. They lack a sense of journey with key milestones and targets. Ensure the plan answers the three questions: who, what and why?

Embed your plan in your day-to-day activities: for example, within your regular status report format. It needs to have as much prominence as the various day-to-day projects on which you are working, and should not be an annual plan that gets dusted down the night before the internal review meeting.

Have a client/supplier audit: whether it is a fully comprehensive survey carried out by third party or a series of client interviews conducted by a senior person from inside your company (but who does *not* work on the business day to day), it is vital that you have an honest and rounded picture of your company's performance and role in the client's eyes. It is also an opportunity to explore the extent and nature of any future work.

Get senior management to celebrate and reward success: as they do with new client wins.

Deal with fear and jealousy: if you're worried that another department in your company may screw up and thus jeopardize your own existing client relationship, you must alert senior management – it is their responsibility to make the call about what to do.

Get your people across the different departments together: so they learn about each other. Help them all to understand the different specialist expertise within the organization and in what circumstances it can help their clients.

Train your people: on the soft skills as well as on technical knowledge. There's nothing "harder" or more commercially profitable or more effective in driving organic growth.

Build in time for teams to gel as real teams: be creative in the ways you can build *esprit de corps* and factor in sufficient time for the individuals to cohere as a whole.

Debrief: after the client meeting, get everyone together to review your performance, learn from the experience and work out what needs to happen next.

Being more effective with and helpful to your clients

Thus far we've looked at why organic growth is valuable, what good practice looks like, what better practice delivers, the internal barriers to achieving organic growth and how to overcome them, and how companies can prepare themselves better in order to make organic growth more likely to happen.

We now turn our attention to clients:

> What are the different phases of a client/adviser relationship?

> How do you ensure you keep the relationship fresh and vital?

> Are you spending the right amount of time with the right clients?

> How to communicate better with clients.

> How to think about clients' business issues more creatively.

> How to structure meetings with clients about organic growth opportunities.

> How to use questions to generate better understanding and guide conversations.

> When to have the conversation.

> Putting it all into practice.

9

The three different phases of business relationships

Much of what we discuss in this book is designed to help individuals and companies to become more self-aware – more conscious of what they are doing in pursuit of organic growth. We aim to help you stand back and see what's really going on, or what needs to go on. By holding up a mirror to current behaviour and showing the most effective ways to act, we intend to get people to think about how they can improve the results they are getting.

In this chapter we examine the subject of relationships with clients: how they work, what makes them go sour, and how to keep them strong. In order to grow the business your firm has with its existing clients, the relationship must be strong because strong relationships are the essential bedrock of all your activity. Your client audit scores will reveal how strong your relationships are now, but we need to look at ways of spotting a relationship that's going bad and, just as importantly, what to do about it.

Human relations

Personal relationships, such as between two people who are married, or professional relationships between client and professional adviser, all undergo three distinct phases:

Phase 1 – Courtship
Phase 2 – Being in love
Phase 3 – Maturity

Phase 1 – Courtship

In the business relationship cycle, Phase 1, courtship, is all about the new-business chase. The drama of the pitch process culminates in the client agreeing to "go out" with one company, having been chased by many potential suitors. In the courtship phase, both parties have all their senses on red alert. Every care and attention is paid to every single detail in order to convey the most suitable and appropriate image. The two parties are in a heightened sense of awareness about themselves and each other – what signals of encouragement or discouragement are being given and received. It is akin to a speed date – a short and intense period of time when each must convey exactly the right signals in order to win the prize.

The eyes are watching – does the other party look good, look right? Do I look right? How are they behaving – warm or cold, receptive or indifferent? The ears are tuned to pick up every little nuance – you actually listen, very intently, to everything the other person says. Your entire armoury of senses is utilized at maximum strength in order to win the heart, mind, body and soul of your potential partner.

The professional new-business pitcher focuses intently on the target client to engender the same level of rapport that the suitor aims for with his date. Every clue garnered from the use of the senses – including the sixth sense! – is turned to advantage in helping the prospective client to choose him rather than the competitors.

And once the courtship ritual is decided, the relationship moves into Phase 2 – Being in love.

Phase 2 – Being in love

Normally, in the period immediately following the appointment of a new adviser to a client, there is a small but noticeable dip in the extreme level of attention that the suitor has been paying to the other person. This is most probably due to the exhaustion of being on full display all the time over the preceding few weeks of the courtship. But after this, the relationship goes into exponential mode – it just soars up the S curve in a near-vertical trajectory. This is called being in love.

After a new-business win, both the client and the supplier act like two people in love with each other. Eager to please and eager to encourage, adviser and client are excited about the possibilities promised in their relationship. For the adviser, nothing is too much trouble. Over-servicing the client is the norm in this phase. The team are gushing with ideas and enthusiasm and tackle every task with gusto. They put the client's previous advisers in the shade in terms of responsiveness and proactivity. At the adviser's company there is no shortage of bright, gifted people to work on this client's business. This client is the hot client of the moment – on whose behalf exciting work is happening – and so attracts more than its fair share of attention within the organization. It is the new wife in the harem.

In return, the client feels delighted and well disposed towards his new partner. The new ideas and initiatives brought to the client are welcomed. Some of them are implemented. Some of them are implemented quickly! This encourages the adviser more and the level of service goes up and up. And because this new client pays its bills on time, things go from strength to strength and everybody is happy.

Phase 3 – Maturity

It is well known that you have to work at making a marriage work year after year. Marriages need nurturing because mature relationships can either grow stronger with the passing of time or they can weaken. You can go from strength to strength or you can get stuck in a rut. Mostly, people stuck in a relationship rut mirror exactly their professional counterparts who have reached a hiatus in their business relationship: they go into what psychiatrists call denial. They ignore the symptoms of a declining relationship. They turn a blind eye or ignore the multiplicity of clues that things are just not what they used to be, that things are not right in this relationship. And there is normally an abundance of clues to suggest that things are going off the rails:

> you're spending less time with each other than you used to;

> the time you do spend together is spent arguing;

> habits and the other party's ways of behaving start to grate;

> little things start to annoy: neither of you feels you are getting much from the relationship, so anger and resentment start to fester.

In business relationships, the client often feels that the professional adviser has downgraded the team working on the business, or that the top management don't seem to be available for meetings as often as they were. They feel that the quality of work and ideas has slipped; that the same old problems keep recurring; that phone calls aren't returned promptly. (This last point is a massive bone of contention for clients.)

The negative side of Phase 3 happens when partners who were formerly in love start to take each other for granted. **Taking each other for granted kills off many a marriage.** And it kills business relationships faster than anything else.

Interestingly, although this seems intuitive, it is not often recognized by professional service companies. A survey conducted by the Bay Group among accountancy firms and their clients (CFOs and financial managers) looked at the disparity between the reasons cited by the two sides for relationship breakdown.

In the 2006 survey 47% of practising accountants were under the impression that they lose clients owing to "price, fees, costs, budgets and affordability". But finance managers and CFOs have a totally different perspective. *Of these, 79% cited "poor client service and a lack of attentiveness" as the number-one reason for relationship breakdown with their suppliers.* Service was felt to be only the third most important reason among the accountancy firms.

The CFO/financial manager clients ranked the reasons for firing their accountants as follows:

79%	Poor client service and lack of attentiveness.
66%	Price, fees, costs, budgets and affordability.
38%	Not getting enough time with accountancy firm's best people.
34%	Bad chemistry.
33%	Lack of proactive advice.
22%	The need for new or different services.

Source: Bay Street Group, 2006

Mismatched client assessments of what they want in terms of attention and service and what they perceive is being delivered are the rocks on which most adviser/ client relationships founder. So, to start with, revisit your service provision agreement and check that what you promised and agreed to deliver is actually being delivered.

Ensuring you avoid the Phase 3 relationship rut

The key to keeping long-running relationships strong is to keep on injecting them with doses of energy. You need to keep putting in energy so that you propel the relationship into an even steeper Phase 2 curve just at the moment when it looks as if it might trail off into decline.

The moment you suspect your client relationship might be slipping into decline, take immediate action to re-energize it:

> offer to repitch the business;
> give the client a free pitch on some aspect of their business;
> recommend a relationship audit;
> be self-critical: how could you improve and change for the better?;
> implement – actually improve and change for the better;
> refresh your team: bring in new blood (you'll get new ideas and new energy);
> relaunch your company to the client;
> give the client a free brainstorm with your company's top talent.

Do something that signals hunger and keenness. Give your client the business equivalent of a second honeymoon.

But the best way of insuring yourself against slipping into Phase 3 is to ask yourself every day: *Why should my client do business with me today? How am I going to make a difference to my client today?* It is a vital question to ask every day for a number of reasons:

1 We have no divine right to work with any of our clients. If we no longer make a difference to them or their company's performance we are redundant. As they were fond of saying in *The Godfather*, this is "strictly business". We must assume that we cannot rely on favours or goodwill.

2 Clients have an ever-increasing level of expectation in terms of the delivery they demand, and that ever-increasing level of expectation represents an opportunity for our competitors. It is comparatively easy to make an existing professional services adviser look slovenly, slow and off the pace when it comes to client service and proactivity if you are a circling predator targeting a particular client. The client's expectation of their knowledge level is lower than it is for an existing adviser, so they cut them more slack and are absolutely bowled over if they exhibit more insight than expected. The predatory team is often composed of the very finest brains and the most dynamic operators – people who are both compelling and very buyable. Contrast this with your tired old team beaten up by years of working with this client – a team that no longer visibly relishes every contact with the client, who is, even now, being seduced by your competitor's new-business A team.

3 Clients are people too and they enjoy being made to feel special just like anyone else. It is difficult to look dynamic and fresh throughout a relationship, so it is much easier for an interloper to make himself look attentive and energetic by comparison.

Only by earning our stripes every day can we guard

against the natural lethargy that creeps into an ongoing client relationship. And in order to earn our stripes every day we need to be prodded into being attentive and dynamic – better to prod ourselves every morning than to arrive at our desk, log on to our computer and find the client equivalent of a "Dear John" email waiting for us. Beware: professional seducers are out there in force and they are very good. They are probably talking to your client right now, offering him a new piece of research, a novel view of his market, an innovative new product, an in-depth study of his competitors – all irresistible bait to your client.

The only way to guard against them is to assess your own position by asking: how will we prove today that our client is with the right team?

The auditor's tale

AuditComCo is a company that specializes in auditing the marketing communications of major advertisers. They provide both benchmark data and bespoke advice relating to the effectiveness and efficiency of their clients' marketing and communications expenditure.

Richard was the newly installed chief executive. With his board, he established that their strong position in the UK market was likely to be at best stable, at worst in decline, under attack from competitors and the relentless downward pressure on margins. They concluded that they needed to grow their nascent international business. In this they were helped by two factors.

There was a general trend towards globalization among the major advertisers – the rate of change was variable but the direction was clear: local decisions were being superseded by regional, regional by global. Second, AuditComCo could realize their ambitions by growing their business from within the stable of their existing clients, many of whom had global or regional operations.

Therefore, their strategy was to build on these beginnings to develop a growth plan that leveraged and built on their existing client relations in order to grow a truly international business. In effect, organic growth was their route to the future.

Their first key action was to create their own global structure, appointing global account directors (GADs) to their key clients, and a team of locally/regionally based executives to support them, together charged with realising AuditComCo's ambition. This was, of course, a disruption – past interrelationships were changed, perspectives were new and life was less comfortable.

This could be regarded as standard practice; but they did employ one unusually valuable tactic – reciprocity. This meant that GAD A (say in the USA) responsible for client A might have GAD B (in the UK) working in their support team, but that GAD B would have GAD A working in their team on client B.

The principle was that this reciprocity would encourage positive interdependencies so that both GADs A and B would realize that if they worked together their chances would be enhanced; but that if one did not pull their weight then it was more than likely that their counterpart would also not be fully supportive. By and large this worked. But Richard commented that it could take as much as a year for people to commit; and some didn't even after twelve months. They soon left the company to be replaced by people who understood that an international perspective was the winning formula for the company and for themselves! Interestingly many of these new recruits were not specialist auditors, but came from a range of client-facing roles from various sectors.

The second step was to "to apply the processes of new business to developing our existing business". This was to ensure that their efforts were, again in Richard's words, "planned, more efficient and proactive – not chaotic and anarchic".

They spent time and money finding a suitable and effective toolkit to help map their clients. As anyone who has worked internationally will know, supposedly simple organizational structures disguise a reality of confusion, dotted lines, distractions and contradictions. Even in the most simple structure a global director is likely to have three (or more) regional reports, who in turn have their own teams, who in turn have to work with national teams; all this is complicated by the presence of Procurement and budget-holders, both again working at global, regional or local levels.

AuditComCo decided to develop their own proprietary relationship mapping system. "We needed to know who could say yes or no, who held the budget, who gave technical or general management approval and the interaction between all these people. Essentially who had authority over what and whom, and who else had influence."

They then developed a set of arguments to demonstrate how and why they could be of (added) value to the client. They had innumerable rational arguments, supporting case histories, testimonials and research initiatives – all these demonstrated their expertise.

But their main angle of attack was how they and their

services would save their clients time and above all money. Crude, yes, over-simple, yes, and effective – of course. But it addressed one of the biggest problems that all international organizations face: the duplication – sometimes triplication! – of effort as global overlaps with local. This is particularly true of organizations moving through the process of globalization, when the costs of the new processes are compounded by the costs of the legacy systems that linger.

Their pitch to their clients became: "this is how we can save you money (and time); this is how you can meet your own international commitments and, so, this is how you will become a hero".

The results of their restructure, their dedication to understanding their clients and their focus on the benefits of their offer (rather than the merits of their expertise) resulted in AuditComCo changing their business profile dramatically. They retained their UK base but increased their international business from below 20% to over 70%.

We applaud their leadership – significant rather than incremental organic growth invariably happens from the top – and their focus on the real benefits they offered their clients. We recognize too that their approach demanded significant internal reorganization without which their plan would have foundered.

Key lessons

> Your clients' ambitions are the means for your own growth.

> Restructuring may be necessary. This is painful and takes time.

> Develop proprietary client knowledge systems.

> Create compelling arguments as to why a client should give you more of their business.

10
Spend more time with the right clients

In the post-dot-com recession that hit the marketing communications industry in the early part of the 2000s, there was a striking correlation between the companies that continued to perform well financially in those difficult years, and the companies where no one seemed to be in the office. The performing companies were empty not because everyone had been laid off, but because everyone was down at the clients' offices seeking out opportunities and ways to help their clients – clients who were also experiencing tough market conditions. Those companies that didn't perform so well through the recession were notably more replete with staff sitting at their workstations. Staff who were busy looking busy so they wouldn't be made redundant! Staff who were hunkering down in fear for their jobs rather than getting into the trenches with their clients.

In a study conducted by the Remsen Group published in 2006 (*Individual Marketing Efforts, Selling Professional Services*), in response to the question: *"Which of the following marketing tactics has your law firm found to be the most effective at generating new revenue"*, websites, newsletters, collateral material, bylined articles, speeches and seminars accounted for only 27%. By far the biggest contributor was seen as "visiting clients", which received 61%. There is simply no better way to unlock revenue than to spend time face to face with clients, having a structured and meaningful dialogue about their needs and requirements – ideally when you have a specific way of helping in mind; but as is so often the case, just by being there with them, opportunities to help arise. As Woody Allen said: "80% of success is just showing up."

A PR company was told by its client that they had no budget for the coming year and so no public relations activity would occur. The PR company offered to second one of their staff to the client's offices three days a week – so the client had a resource to use should the need arise. Within four months this person had produced €1 million of income for the PR company. And this from a company that had said sixteen weeks before that they had no budget! People kept coming up to her and asking whether she knew how they might do so and so, or whether she could help them with this project they had to complete. Being there is important. It puts you in a position where you can help.

Where are you and your company spending your time? And are you spending your time profitably? Looking at a study into the amount of time companies were spending with their clients of different revenue levels, it is telling how small clients absorb such a disproportionate amount of their advisers' time:

Client monthly revenue	% clients	% revenue	% visits	% profits
More than $100k	6%	28%	11%	38%
$50k–100k	16%	48%	17%	52%
$25–50k	30%	14%	38%	8%
Less than $25k	48%	10%	34%	2%

(Source: Learning International)

As a boss of ours used to say, "Shoot where the ducks are flying!" Make sure you are focusing effort on the areas of highest profit potential, not frittering away your valuable time with those clients who do not have the potential to affect your company's financial performance but who soak up your time and are habitually over-serviced. And if you're over-servicing the small clients, you'll be under-servicing the big clients – the clients who will affect your fortunes. And that is a very dangerous territory to be in.

Another reason you need to be down at your clients' offices as frequently as possible is that you need to cover all the bases. All too often professional service companies are overly reliant on one or two deep relationships within a client organization and are not entrenched more broadly. This leaves them exposed and vulnerable if one of their key relationships goes sour or if that contact moves out of the client organization. It is therefore imperative to cultivate numerous touch points within a client organization. Apart from the bulwark this provides against the threat of a few key relationships being severed, it is also a recognition of the complexity of decision-making within most client organizations. If you are fortunate, you may have just one client decision-maker who can determine whether or not you get more work from his department or organization. Far more frequently, there are many people within the client organization who influence the decision to buy.

Customer size by employees	Average no. of decision influencers	No. visited by sales staff
Less that 200	3.43	1.72
200–400	4.85	1.75
401–1,000	5.81	1.90
1,000+	6.50	1.65

Source: Learning International

This survey shows that the average client company employing over 1,000 staff will have 6.5 people who influence each purchase decision. And yet of those 6.5 people, only 1.65 receive a visit from the company selling its services to that client organization. Clearly, this means that the majority of influencers have no contact with the company trying to sell its services.

Audit yourself on your key clients

1 How much time are you spending *thinking about* your client's business as opposed to *doing* your work on the client's business?

2 Which clients are receiving most of your attention? Are they the right clients to be focusing on?

3 Where are you on the relationship curve? What independent evidence do you have from your most recent client relationship audit which verifies or contradicts your assumption?

4 How many touch points do you have within the client organization? Which are the strongest? Where are you most vulnerable?

5 What were the last three proactive initiatives you took to the client? With what level of success?

6 How often does your boss/your most senior management meet your client? What resulted from the last meeting?

7 When did you win this client? Are they obliged to run a pitch in the next eighteen months?

8 What new blood have you introduced to your team to revitalize your client relationship?

9 What do you know about your clients personally? What sort of people are they? What are they interested in outside work?

10 If you were pitching for this client as a competitor to your company, what would you be doing differently? How would you be behaving? How can you re-engage all your senses and put renewed energy into revitalizing your client partnership?

11

How to communicate better with clients

All business is ultimately about people. There can be no more rewarding enterprise than the study of our fellow humans; not so we can manipulate or control them, but so we can communicate better with them, get better at understanding each other and help our respective businesses to thrive.

Our hero, Dale Carnegie, knew instinctively that people buy people. And generally, people buy from people they like and respect, and they generally don't buy from people they don't like and don't respect. And whereas in love it is often said that opposites attract, in business this rule very rarely applies.

The art of working with clients is to understand them as well as their business needs, and to be able to couch your advice and proposals in terms that they find comfortable and acceptable. It is important to understand that there are people out there who think about and see the world very differently from you.

Understanding what you are like and how you

communicate is just the beginning of generating good and profitable relationships. You must also seek to understand others and then couch your recommendations to them in a style and manner that engender rapport rather than conflict.

There are many different tools with which to analyse your own and other people's communication styles: the Belbin Survey, Myers Briggs and a host of psychometric profiling techniques. Use any of them and you'll achieve better communication with your clients. Find the system that works for you.

We happen to use a very simple system which uses a behavioural-style matrix for four basic types of people. The system divides the world into those who are driven primarily by the relationship and those who are focused more on the specific task, and into those who prefer to ask and those who prefer to tell. Although there are shades of difference both between and within these types, broadly they are described as:

Expressives – relationship-oriented people who are driven by ideas, particularly their own!

Amiables – relationship people who like to consult others and ask their opinion.

Drivers – task-oriented people who prefer to lead and tell others what to do.

Analyticals – task-related people who like to weigh up evidence objectively and ask questions.

Broadly speaking, Expressives and Drivers, when

confronted, will fight their corner. When pushed, Expressives will go on the attack, whereas Drivers will get more and more insistent and dictatorial. Amiables and Analyticals will run from conflict, which they find unhelpful and difficult. Amiables will seek compromise, not confrontation, in the face of resistance; Analyticals will seek to avoid conflict by going back to the facts. Being able to spot which type you are dealing with in any given situation will help you communicate more empathetically with the different types of clients you encounter.

Why does all this matter? It helps you to work out how to behave with the different styles. And because you know your client, you'll be able to work out his or her style. Once you're more aware of your client's personality profile, it might help explain why certain approaches you make work well, and why others don't work as well.

Below are some simple do's and don'ts for when you communicate with someone from each type.

Expressives

DO

> Be open, friendly and enthusiastic.

> Establish your credibility quickly.

> Emphasize results, possibilities, quick wins, actions.

> Be on time (they'll be late).

> Invest time in the relationship with regular contact.

> Get written commitments.

DON'T

> Get into technical details (they get bored easily).

> Write an introductory letter.

> Rush the discussion.

> Mistake enthusiasm for commitment.

> Forget that they will be showing the same level of enthusiasm to your competitor.

Amiables

DO

> Be open, honest, sincere and punctual.

> Expect to share personal information.

> Support their feelings and position.

> Summarize their key issues.

> Tell them why this is the right solution.

DON'T

> Be threatening or corner them.

> Rush things.

> Expect lots of factual information immediately.

> Forget that they are difficult to move from an incumbent supplier.

> Be cool and aloof.

Drivers

DO

> Have concise, documented evidence which stresses results, competence, effectiveness, quality, flexibility and action.

> Be formal, on time and succinct.

> Let them talk – it will be relevant.

> Keep questions factual.

> Give them options.

DON'T

> Waste their time on small talk.

> Try to compete or take control.

> Tell them, give opinions or recommendations.

> Overdo the detail.

> Go for all or nothing.

Analyticals

DO

> Send an agenda beforehand and ask for feedback.

> Be on time and very well prepared with documented facts and evidence of accuracy and quality.

> Be tangible and practical.

> List pros and cons logically (they like order).

> Demonstrate how you are minimizing risks for them.

DON'T

> Be late, disorganized and messy, casual, loud, vague or too informal.

> Offer personal special incentives (e.g. hospitality). They are too businesslike to use them and would worry what their colleagues would think if they did.

> Threaten. Fear will not work.

> Forget to take notes: they won't tell you twice.

> Forget to follow up on action points or commitments quickly.

12

Thinking more creatively about clients' business issues

When you begin thinking more about a client's business, you need to look at their issues in a number of different ways and to stimulate your creativity. Although you could closet yourself away for two hours every week like Rodin's statue *The Thinker*, there are lots of other ways to generate ideas and opportunities.

> Read the client's website and company literature: it's amazing how few people working for a company do this, and you will almost certainly identify new angles or issues the company really isn't addressing well, or at all.

> Read your client's competitors' websites.

> Visit the front line: if they sell their products and services to consumers, visit their outlets and their competitors' outlets.

> Become a customer; buy their product or service and learn from the experience. Do the same with their competitors.

> Work behind the counter for a day serving their public

and asking them questions about your client's products and services.

> Go to a trade show or exhibition.

> Attend industry/sector conferences and seminars.

> Accompany their sales force on the road.

> Read the trade and business press every day (*FT*, *The Economist*): it's always full of news and information about your clients, their market, their competitors.

> Conduct some research.

> Convene an expert panel comprised of commentators from different disciplines.

> Read the latest business books.

> Use lateral-thinking techniques like Edward De Bono's "Six thinking hats".

> Brainstorm with your colleagues who *don't* work on this client.

And here's another tool that might help you look at your client's issues from new angles. It's called **PECSTEL**, and is a checklist of perspectives that can provide new insights into any business.

Political (internal and external)

Economic (macro/micro economic and financial issues affecting the client's business)

Customer & competition (trends and activity)

Socio-demographic (social and population trends affecting performance in the future)

Technology (impact on sector and players)

Environmental (threats and opportunities)

Legislative (threats and opportunities emanating from regulators, domestic parliaments or supranational bodies)

Looking through different lenses at the world and how it might affect your client's business can be a very lucrative way (for both you and the client) to spend your two hours a week. Looking at different scenarios and what they might entail for the client's business will reveal a multitude of different possibilities – both threats and opportunities – and if they have been provided or hosted by your firm, it puts you in a key strategic position in the client's overall supplier base.

This form of exercise is basic scenario planning. Examples of the sorts of issues that might emerge are given below.

Political

Political trends and the issues they create with customers have direct implications for the style and manner in which business is conducted. Analysing these key political dynamics can produce new and more appropriate ways of doing business with clients and deliver your clients competitive advantage.

Economic and financial

In business we tend to focus on very short-term issues. Usually we're focused on just getting through this week's, or even today's, workload. We worry about the payback for this solitary deal, or this particular project. But to focus exclusively on the short term ignores some economic trends that are very slow but extremely powerful.

For example: what are the implications for the labour markets in our clients' organizations and our own? In five years' time, what will the graduate intake of your company look like? Likely as not it will be far more international, cosmopolitan and diverse than it is now. Our fragile, relatively closed system is facing huge upheaval and challenge. If our clients start moving their employees across different markets and expect them to be fluent in two or three languages and familiar with as many cultures, how should you be staffing your team in order to reflect this change?

Customers and competitors

With customers demanding not just service but service plus, and at reduced fee levels (i.e. more for less), what can you offer to generate higher perceived value to your clients? This shift to service plus is increasingly widespread. The aero engine manufacturer GE, for example, no longer sells mere engines. Instead, it sells contracts for successful flight hours. This means it provides engines plus monitoring equipment to predict when the engines will need servicing, and staff to provide that servicing. GE's airline customers like this proposition because it makes their lives easier so that they can focus on *their* clients – the airline's passengers.

What implications does the service-plus trend have for your offer and also for your clients' business? How can you bundle your or their products and services together to provide enhanced value? For example, you might be in a business that charges clients to manage a crisis – something has gone wrong, they are being sued, they have had a product recall, they are under attack from a pressure group, their financial results are being questioned. But you could also offer your ability to pre-empt such crises. In this way, you can move from being merely valuable *in* a crisis to a more proactive and regular relationship *before* any crisis emerges.

Socio-demographics

People used to sort themselves by neighbourhood, or trade union, or other such groupings. Now there are many, many new groupings which have become increasingly important over the last few years – vested-interest groups such as the UK's Countryside Alliance; issue groups such as the anti-Iraq war protest movement; virtual groups such as Friends Reunited and MySpace. What implications are there for your clients? What's going on behind the groupings?

For example: street protests by pensioners might easily be dismissed in the UK, but in the USA the largest lobbying group of all is the American Association of Retired Persons, the AARP. It has an enormous effect on policy over a wide range of issues: pensions, healthcare, vehicle design, cable television prices, investment practices, and so on.

What is your client's strategy towards these powerful and influential groups? What threats and opportunities do they bring in the service area that you provide? And what new groupings might be coming, and with what cost to your clients?

Technology

The Internet has given easy access to a whole range of expertise and advisory services over the last few years. Does this devalue your role or enhance it? How can technology be harnessed to give you not just a *high-trust* reputation with your clients but also a *high-speed* way of delivering better service?

Sometimes there's a tsunami of new technology – mobile phones, the Internet, BlackBerries. What could the next technology be – more blitzkrieg change or a slow consolidation of what exists already?

Environment

What is the next big thing? What will help selling techniques? The rapid adoption by governments and businesses of green policies and points of view about global warming and becoming carbon neutral could affect your and your client's ability to do business if you are off the pace on these issues. From an almost insignificant side debate three or more years ago, environmental issues have stormed the economic and political stage, with a raft of legislation trailing in their wake. What do you need to do? What do your clients need to do?

Legislative

There may be very overt costs for your clients' businesses in the legislative arena (e.g. compliance with such regulatory laws as Sarbanes Oxley) and a host of other, less obvious and low-visibility threats. Keeping a watchful eye on the regulatory environment, the domestic legislature and the supranational bodies can produce a catalogue of needs for clients – and therefore work for your company. So watch the people watching you!

Ten top tips from clients

We meet clients every day. And we never miss a chance to ask them what they want from their professional service suppliers. Here we share some of the answers we hear consistently. Even if you believe you know what your clients want, it never hurts to be reminded.

1   **Proactivity: "From so many of our advisers all we hear is "what do you want?" over and over. What we *want* to hear is : "To achieve what you want, here's what you should do and why and how'. If you inspire me, you'll become my consultant not just my supplier."**

There are a number of clichés which get trotted out by professional service firms which sound great but rarely stand up to much scrutiny. "We're highly innovative" and "We pride ourselves on our proactivity with our clients" are the two most common. But what about the follow-up evidence? If you say you're innovative, what can you show to prove this claim? What evidence of intelligent innovation within your field or on any client business can you demonstrate? As ever, claims without proof are just corporate puffery – so much hot air. And being proactive has to be backed up by examples, examples that demonstrate effort above and beyond the normal day-to-day client service or just getting the job done. Going above and beyond the call of duty is what will differentiate the experience of dealing with your firm from dealing with any of your competitors.

We all know that individuals who make that extra effort to help us (i.e. are proactive in management jargon) enhance our view of their company tenfold. Again and again we hear stories of day-to-day heroics from the staff of truly great companies: Tesco staff members who chase around to help a customer who asks for a particular product that is out of stock on the shopfloor, but go and fetch it and take it to that customer at the checkout when a delivery comes in; customer careline staff who make it their personal mission to sort out your problem without passing you from one anonymous call centre operative to another. When you come across these people they exhibit the mentality that proclaims proactivity. They are such a pleasure to meet – but they're rare, which is why we tell all our friends about them!

2   **Understand the environment the client works in: "Be practical in your approach; be speedy! Give us input early. Make us look good! Be cost and time flexible."**

Clients work under enormous time and cost pressures: they need help in getting ideas adopted internally, and you can help not only by providing better answers but by thinking about how that answer can be best delivered. Think behind the brief you're working on – what client-side politics might be at play? How is your client/client's division/client's company performing at the moment? What is the client's company culture? What really matters to your client? What must you fight for and what is easy to compromise on or trade? Being precious or slow when the client needs pragmatism and speed – which he will quite a lot of the time – is damaging. Be timely – know when to be firm and when to bend. Help the client to shine in any way you can ... and do it with urgency and in a language that his company will appreciate and understand.

3 **"Visit the front line regularly."**

Don't stay in an ivory tower. Even if you're a highfalutin lawyer, if your client has shops, shop there. If your client makes soap, wash with it. Do what you can to keep closely involved with your client's business interests. But don't just use their products and services or visit their stores passively. Notice what's going on – what your client's customers are doing and saying. What do you think of the client's products and services? How could they be improved? If you offer your client fresh insight or thoughts about *their business* rather than merely about the bit of their

business you are concerned with, they will listen to
your advice with greater respect and sincerity.

4   **"Clients take soundings from each other."**

In other words, clients talk to each other. They discuss
the relative merits of their suppliers and advisers. They
spread both good and bad news about their
experiences. They ask advice about who to use, who is
hot, who is not. You do not exist in a vacuum. Be
aware! Don't make enemies.

5   **"In a world where increasingly the supplier offer is
basically a commodity, the key rational
differentiator is often difficult to tell. If you're in
the league tables you'll all have the capability. But
over and above these things advice and insight can
really differentiate."**

In all likelihood, you work for a well-regarded firm
within your chosen field of competence. But your
client is spoilt for choice – there's no shortage of
companies that can transact the business you can
transact. But if you've dug deeper, found out more,
used time productively, you'll come up with more
useful answers than the competition. And if you
always talk about the client and his business, not your
company, you'll always be relevant and interesting.
Who do you listen to? Someone who says "this is what
I've found out about you and your business and here's
what I can do to help you with your issue", or
someone who says "here's what I've done for other

people just like you in the past and here are a few general ideas on what might work"? Easy choice. Don't rely on your company's reputation or endless league tables – clients don't believe them anyway. When your company's brightest and best turn up for the client and they've really thought about the client's issues, it'll stand out a mile.

6 **"Help me! Stop trying to flog me your products under cover of a risk review."**

Don't be a cynical salesperson. Whatever the financial pressure. Act sincerely in the client's best interests at all times. Don't think the client is so stupid they won't see your selfish commercial imperative to sell him this or that solution. Be judicious in what you take to your client. All too often professional service firms put huge pressure on their client coverage teams to introduce a weekly barrage of the company's specialist product salespeople in the vain hope that, regardless of what the client needs, if they stick enough stuff under the client's nose, something will get bought. The point of having the client's ear is so you listen precisely to what they need – not so you sell them what you want to sell them. As one client said: "Those advisers who have the patience to build relationships and understand me and my business will be ahead when it comes to decision time."

7 **"Look for a crisis."**

When the chips are down and the client is under huge

stress to perform, to save the day, this is when you can cement your relationship most securely. Crises forge the strongest bonds because they are tempered in the fire of conflict. If you are calm but recognize the need for urgency, give honest counsel, bring bad tidings but remain unshakeably onside, solve the problem *and* act as "humbly as the dust", you will have a client for life. Exhibit unceasing hunger to help and resourcefulness – these are qualities in allies which clients value.

8 **"Numbers are the language of business. Speak fluently."**

All business decisions need to be justified on the basis of financial criteria. Make sure your proposal has a financial rationale behind it. This might be obvious to those of you who are accountants or bankers, but if you cannot read a balance sheet or understand a P&L, don't expect a smooth ride if you're presenting a proposal to the client's board. Wherever and whenever you can, try to put a financial context to the need for your client to act and a financial justification for the action itself. If you speak architecture, marketing, engineering, real estate or law, learn a second language: money.

9 **"Simplify your sell. Eliminate your technical jargon."**

You aren't always dealing with one client. At many times there are a number of clients from different departments or backgrounds who will be involved in the decision. Some will have very strong technical skills in the discipline you represent, others might have no knowledge or familiarity with the terminology of your discipline. You must accommodate them all. If you're a lawyer or corporate banker talking about the complexities of a pension fund, then it is safe to assume that the client's chief treasurer and CFO will understand every word you say. But what about the client's trade union representative? Make sure you are crystal clear about what it is that you are asking the client team to approve – not just crystal clear to you, but to *all* of them as well.

10 "Relationships cut right across supply chain management."

Client organizations need objective and strategic criteria by which they appoint their advisers and business partners. The intention behind these criteria is to remove subjectivity and personal relationships from the decision-making process. While this is admirable, ultimately, when companies buy professional services, they are buying people. We've met many clients who tell us, off the record, that while they go through the logical and objective selection process (because they have to), they all too often know exactly who they want to use, regardless of the procurement process protocols in place. If they can give the job to someone they know and trust, then objectivity is sacrificed to personal judgement.

13
Organizing your thinking: the NISE framework

Once you have gone through the process of thinking about the client's business you need to decide on a handful of key issues to bring to the client's attention. We recommend you fix a meeting dedicated to talking through these issues and these issues alone. If you try to have a conversation on strategic issues at the end of a regular workflow meeting, you will run out of time, the issues will never get a hearing and all your effort will go to waste.

We suggest you aim for one dedicated strategic meeting with the senior client per quarter. Obviously, the onus is on you to make this meeting both stimulating and compelling – it is no good investing the time if it doesn't lead to action by the client. And we suggest that you use the meeting to update your client briefly on any relevant information about your company that they need to know.

Every meeting, especially one as important as this one, needs a structure. And we believe that an appropriate structure for this strategic meeting is summed up in the acronym: NISE

News about your company that the client should know: papers that you have published, events that you are holding, awards or industry recognition that you have received, new clients, senior personnel who have joined or taken on new and relevant responsibilities in the firm. This should be a very sharp and succinct part of the presentation – we don't want to waste time talking about ourselves when we should be talking about the client's business.

It does seem very strange, however, that companies seem to present their credentials only to new business prospects. Why not to your existing clients as well? If you don't, your clients' intelligence about your company is pickled in aspic at the time you were appointed. And as they will be seeing many credentials presentations from your competitors, they will probably know more about these companies than they do about yours. This is not good for business. How can your clients refer other business colleagues to you if they don't know (a) what else you can do and (b) whether you're winning or losing in your own marketplace? Just like all of us, clients appreciate knowing they're working with winners and they need to be kept abreast of all you can do for them. But do be brief!

Issues about the client's business. This is the main substance of the meeting. It's where you and your team focus the client's attention on the two or three most pressing issues that concern them with reference to your company's capabilities and on which they need to either take action or think about taking action. It is the point at which the collective value of all those two hours per week thinking about the client's business, the rigorous **PECSTEL** analysis, the brainstorms, the intelligence you've gathered in the field, etc., comes to the table in edited and compelling form. This is where you devote most time in the meeting and where you help the client understand the need to do something about the situation.

Services that could add value. It is very unlikely that the client is fully aware of everything you can do for them. This is your opportunity to familiarize the client with service areas they currently do not use, new service or product lines that your company now offers, and to ask them for their views on innovations you could make that would improve the service you provide. Case studies, provided they are succinct, relevant and interestingly presented, can be used. Or invite an expert on a particular area to the meeting to present insights you know your client will appreciate.

Extra. We believe that you should always aim to provide the client with something, however small, which adds to the value you provide. It might be a book or an article you've written or read recently and think would interest them. It might be a thoughtful piece of information that you know they will value – perhaps something personal about a hobby or interest of theirs. Or it might be to invite them to celebrate the anniversary of the date on which they awarded your company their business. But do something that shows you genuinely care.

If the meeting goes particularly well – and we mean really well – you can always ask the client whether, knowing your company well (and now even better since you've just updated them), they can think of anyone else in their own organization, or in business generally, who might have a need for your services. Yes, it's a bit cheeky, but it might just produce a lead (remember the Preacher?). Alternatively, you could ask whether the client will give your company a testimonial. They'll usually invite you to write it for them and then sign it on their own letterhead. And you can post it up in your company's reception area as more evidence that your company's clients value what you do for them (which, in turn, is massively reassuring for your other clients).

14

How to use questions to identify your clients' real needs

Your NISE meeting should stimulate debate and lots of discussion. Although you will present your observations, ideas and opinions, you can also use the opportunity to quiz the client on his views and concerns. Knowing how to use questions well is an invaluable skill. Questions are the rudder with which you steer your conversations with the client – they can be used to elicit information, clarify meaning, establish motives, reveal concerns and gain commitment. There are different types of question, each with a specific purpose.

> I keep six honest serving men
> They taught me all I know
> Their names are What and Why and When
> And How and Where and Who.
>
> *(Rudyard Kipling)*

Open questions

These are designed to open debate and to get your client talking about the issues you need to discuss and their relevance to them.

Examples:

> How's business?

> What are the issues in your business right now?

> What are the areas you think can be improved?

> Which competitors are you concerned about today?

Closed questions

These questions are used to pin down specifics in the discussion, to confirm views and to clarify meaning.

Examples:

> Is that an issue that needs attention right now?

> Do you want to focus on X or Y today?

Fact-finding questions

This category of questions is designed to find out facts and specific, objective information. Such questions use the open forms of what, how, who, where and when, and add the words "exactly", "specifically" or "precisely".

Examples:

> How exactly do you measure success?

> What exactly do you mean by good?

> When specifically do you need this?

> Who specifically is involved in this decision?

> You said everything was fine. What precisely did you mean by that?

Motivation-finding questions

These questions should be used to establish the decision-maker's motivations and criteria. They use the words "what" or "how" and add the word "you".

Examples:

> What made you decide to ...?

> What prevents you from ...?

> What's important to you about ...?

> What makes you believe ...?

> How will you decide ...?

> How do you feel about ...?

The essence of good questioning technique is to keep drilling (in a charming, non-confrontational but persistent manner) and to get specific answers. Do not be satisfied with vague statements and generalities – they will get you nowhere.

By using questions properly, you will be able to build a picture in the client's head of what the issues are and why he needs to act. You will also steer the conversation in a logical way towards a solution.

The marketing services tale

Françoise is the CEO of the EMEA operations of a major global marketing services group, MarcomCo. The operating companies work in a large number of sectors: sponsorship, healthcare, direct marketing, digital, public relations. Each agency reports to its own network HQ but also has strong dotted-line responsibility to Françoise and her regional team, who in turn represent the ultimate and only shareholder.

This is the classic matrix management structure, balancing the needs and priorities of the shareholder with those of the individuality of each operating company.

Françoise is convinced of the importance of organic growth. "It is the most profitable as well as being the most professionally satisfying type of work." Indeed, in 2006 MarcomCo achieved over 60% of its double-digit growth from getting more assignments and revenues from existing clients.

"It is more profitable because, compared with new business pitching, organic growth is a more effective and efficient source of growth; and more satisfying because it lies at the very heart of a professional service companies' soul. It is the visible recognition that the client company respects and values the work done and the future relationship."

Françoise divides organic growth into two broad types: what she calls the "do well, do better" strategy and the "inspirational initiative". She describes these as Category 1 and Category 2 opportunities.

By the former, she means the situation where a company does a really outstanding job for its client and gets rewarded by that client by being given either another assignment or the chance to pitch for more work at last.

This is the classic form of organic growth – good work creates more work, or at least more opportunities.

She talked about some obvious accelerators of this process. For example, when good work can be more precisely defined by clear and outstanding financial return on investment (ROI) – so that the successful adviser not only gets more work but an increased share of the budget, as it has been able to demonstrate that its channel and its use of that channel is more effective and efficient than others'.

When asked about the chance of a company expanding its range of services to its existing clients, Françoise was cautious but positive. She argued that it was "difficult to change what was on your business card". In her view, clients tend to put their suppliers into mental boxes from which it is difficult to escape. "You get hired to do a job and it's hard work to develop from that original remit."

As we talked, however, it became clear that the situation was not quite as clear cut. First, some individuals and some companies could and did operate as confidants and advisers in areas beyond their original and natural area(s) of expertise. McKinsey&Company and other management consultants were an obvious example; as were some (individual) bankers and lawyers. Their relationship with their client knew few boundaries and limitations; they were not pigeonholed.

Second, she believed that the partnership model was an effective way of expanding a company's services. This is the model adopted by, for example, lawyers who develop specialist practice areas: M&A, commercial property, intellectual property, and so on. The advantage of this approach, in Françoise's opinion, was that the parent company could offer both expertise via the practice and the relationship glue from the parent.

The second organic growth strategy that she focused on was what she described as the "inspirational initiative" – Category 2 opportunities. These opportunities emerged from a detailed knowledge and understanding of the client's business understanding could only come from an intimacy with the client company and its senior leaders/managers.

She cited two recent examples. One was a telecoms company faced with falling prices and massive customer churn, which therefore needed a more sophisticated and effective customer segmentation programme. The other was an airline whose operational constraints meant that they urgently needed to initiate a more effective and efficient online check-in system to overcome the physical limitations of in-person check-in.

She identified two key principles that could reveal and deliver such growth opportunities.

The first was trust and intimacy with the client. Such a relationship could be personal, based on the relationship between individuals, or could emerge from a more general understanding of the business environment in which the client operated.

In reality, Françoise argued, both intimacies were necessary. A strong personal relationship would allow the client to speak spontaneously about his/her problems: the issues that kept them awake at night and to which there were no obvious or immediate solutions. But intimacy was also important, not only to allow the opening conversation but also to ensure that the proposed solution would get a hearing. The quality of the personal relationship would provide both the opening and the chance to close.

But she also said that opportunities could come from other, less personal relations and knowledge. To this end, she had organized inter-agency workshops where those working on and with a particular client would come together to discuss their work and future opportunities. These workshops had a number of valuable outputs:

1 **All companies were better informed about their counterparts' work and the client – their objectives, the**

issues, the client politics, who knew – or did not know – who ...

2 **The discussion would invariably reveal other simple (Category 1) opportunities**: for example, where one company was doing work towards a client objective but could be helped by and supported by another offering complementary skills.

3 **Third, the workshop could – and did – reveal the bigger Category 2 opportunities**: by sharing information and ideas the agencies were able to construct and see the bigger picture, the totality of the client's business, and not just the narrow and specific area in which they worked.

(As an aside, Françoise did acknowledge that one of the great barriers to organic growth was that too many people today were "business naive". They were more inclined to read their own trade publication than the *Financial Times* or the more general business press. Without such awareness of business, "it was impossible to see things from the perspectives of the CE or the marketing director".)

The second principle was that Françoise had to be totally confident that the company she was recommending to solve the client challenge was able to deliver – that it had a track record and resources that both created confidence in the first place and which ensured that its work, as the project unfolded, would not let the client or her down. She admitted that she was furious with one agency that had been given a number of possible projects but had as yet failed to deliver.

Françoise has one major advantage in this area. As the CEO of a very large group of companies covering the whole spectrum of marketing services and, in many sectors, having three or more active operating companies, she was able to select the ideal partner agency. This meant that she was able to orchestrate both the opportunity and the optimum solution – the right agency (or team of agencies) capable of delivering the right solution.

Françoise is obviously a great supporter of the principles and practices of organic growth. She encourages her operating companies to achieve the highest standards of performance, as she knows that this will naturally create other future opportunities. She does not, however, have line responsibility for the operating companies and therefore can only encourage and cajole.

She puts her own energy into creating and developing cross-group opportunities. She uses her extensive network of senior contacts and general business experience to spot and create opportunities. She organizes and encourages the family of operating companies to cross-fertilize ideas and initiatives. And she believes that no opportunities will be realized without extensive levels of trust – whether personal or corporate, and ideally both – between client and service company, and a clear understanding that past performance is a precondition of future delivery.

Key lessons

> Great work is the vital prerequisite for more work.

> Putting financial value on the results creates even more work.

> Intimacy – corporate and personal – can reveal and seal more opportunities.

> A leader's role is to break down internal silos, create connections and guarantee delivery.

15

How to structure meetings and conversations with clients – the FODA technique

As they say: "It takes two to tango". But someone has to lead. It is your responsibility to lead the **NISE** meeting. In this meeting it is beneficial to follow a logical format used by many effective consultants which will guide the conversation so it moves towards the client taking action on the issues you raise and the advice you give. This is called salesmanship.

Salesmanship tends to get a bad reputation. This is mainly because people associate it with the sharp practices of dubious door-to-door double-glazing salesmen or dodgy second-hand car dealers. People associate salesmanship with foot-in-the-door, flash-talking spivs who try to flog inferior products to people who neither need nor want them – one step away from out-and-out con artists.

While it is true that there are people out there who do behave in this way, their practices are a million miles away from the consultative salesmanship of a true professional. Salesmanship is merely the ability to find out what someone needs and satisfy that need – helping the customer to get what they want. And many of the techniques we've explained in this book help that process to happen in an organized, methodical way.

To understand how consultative selling works, we need to deconstruct the process – first, by showing the four-step process by which you make a compelling case.(This is the sequential process you use to steer the **Issues about the client's business** section of the NISE meeting you're going to have every quarter with your senior client.) And second, by using an illustration of this process in an everyday situation that everyone can relate to – not to trivialize it, but to help you see that it is not difficult or scary; you just need to understand how it works and practise doing it with your clients.

You have reached the stage in the quarterly **NISE** meeting where you wish to reveal to the client the two or three key issues you believe they need to take action on in the next few months. But how do you construct this crucial section of the meeting?

FODA

Facts and evidence about the business situation

Opportunities and consequences resulting from the facts

Desire to do something (not nothing) with *you*

Action necessary to remedy/capitalize on the situation

Facts and evidence

In this section, you present the facts of the situation facing the client's business as you see them.

Opportunities and consequences

In this section you demonstrate the cost of doing nothing about the situation you've identified. How much is the current situation affecting your client's business, and what will happen if it continues or gets worse? These are the scenarios that give context to any recommendation you might put forward.

Desire

Expand the client's desire to buy using evidence of your competence, a special incentive or some sort of additional service which will provide added value.

Action

Only now, once you've been through all the arguments, spelt out the situation, examined the pros and cons of particular scenarios and discussed different strategies for attacking the issue, do you present your recommendation.

Most inexperienced salespeople and all ineffectual sales approaches leap straight from Stage 1 – laying out the facts and evidence – to the last stage. They completely miss out the vital middle stages.

The middle stages are what give **context** to your solution. If you miss them out, you end up in a situation where you've established that there is an issue, but have shown no costs attached to it. It's just another issue, no more or less urgent or tangible than any other issue floating across the client's desk that week. Without a financial context, there's no imperative to take any action. The purpose of the second stage, in particular, is to focus the client's attention on the magnitude of the issue and to make the cost of your proposed solution seem insignificant by comparison.

FODA in practice

Let's take the real example of an organization that specializes in maximizing a client's sales through retail outlets. Based on the very simple premise that "if your product isn't there, it cannot be bought", this company services the business needs of many of the largest manufacturers in Europe and Asia. One of their clients is a very large food company. In the course of their day-to-day work, this field marketing company visits hundreds of retailers a day. They audit what products are on shelf and what products are missing. Then they find out what's preventing those missing products from getting on shelf. For this particular client, they discovered that in a number of outlets owned by one supermarket chain there was a 10% out-of-stock (OOS) problem. That is, 10% of the products that should have been on shelf, weren't.

The field marketing company decided to investigate further, and visited a sample of the stores owned by two other large retailers. In these samples they found average OOS levels of 12% and 15% respectively.

They visited the client and presented the facts. But they didn't then go straight to specifying what would have appeared to the client at this stage to be a very expensive solution – an ongoing compliance audit across a large cross-section of retailers. Instead, they worked through the consequences and opportunities of the situation as it was and ran through some of the monetary implications in different scenarios – what would be the weekly lost sales revenue at different average out-of-stock levels. Every 1% OOS in the three retailers represented a loss of income to the food client of $50,000 per month. So 10% OOS meant the company was losing $0.5 million per month in sales. If this situation continued throughout the next quarter, the food company could lose up to $1.5 million in revenue.

The scenario planning helped the client understand that doing nothing was not an option. And crucially, it gave a robust financial context to the field company's fee proposal for remedying the situation. So the field marketing company sat down with the client team and worked out a solution. And this led to a far larger contract for the field sales team than they had previously had with this client. Not only was it for more work, it was also across the entire portfolio of the client's brands, whereas previously it had been for only one division.

The FODA process leads to BIGGER mandates. Practise it. Use it.

16

The builder's tale – FODA in practice

Let's put this system into an everyday context. Take the example of a builder visiting your home to quote for a job. Let us assume that you want to knock two small rooms into one big space, which you feel will make your home more spacious and light. As the owner of the property, you have several options, one of which is to do this job yourself. You need to weigh up the scale of the task against your capability as a DIY practitioner. If you feel your skills are up to the job, the costs will be minimal – labour is effectively free. The only costs will be a sledgehammer to knock down the dividing wall, some bricks and cement to refashion the space where the wall was, some plaster, some paintbrushes and some paint. All in all, a bill of about \$300. Not much really.

Then the doubts creep in. Are you really good enough to tackle a construction job, even a relatively minor one? You err on the side of caution and decide to call a builder in to estimate for the job.

The builder arrives. He will guide you through an

organized conversation modelled on the **FODA** process. It will go something like this:

He will ask you to tell him what you *want*. You will spell out your vision of the newly remodelled room and how it will look, explaining that it will create more light, that you want it painted white and that you're thinking of putting down bare stripped-oak flooring throughout the entire space. The builder will be listening intently to all your requirements.

He will then go over to the wall in question, the one separating the two rooms. He will stand back from it and examine it from lots of different angles and distances, looking at all the corners, feeling the surfaces, squatting down to examine the skirting boards and the join between the existing carpeted floor and the wall, tapping, knocking and measuring all the surfaces as he assesses the size of the task. He will then go through to the next room and do exactly the same. After this he will go upstairs and look at the space and walls immediately above the rooms you're seeking to join. Finally he'll disappear down to the cellar for a few minutes to look at the job from underneath the two rooms.

Why does he do this? He does this because wants and needs are often totally different things. He has heard what you want, but it is his job, his duty, to show you what you *need*. This is not a casual job. It involves major structural work to your home and it is his next task to help you realize that this is the case.

The builder will now take you through the facts. He will inform you of the materials and style of construction used in this section of the building; he will point out the key areas of stress where the weight is distributed through the existing wall that you want to remove. He will talk of the need to do this job properly in order to preserve the integrity of the brickwork, and he will probably chip away at a small section of the surface to show you how solid the wall is and what a big job this is going to be. He does all this to confront you with the brutal facts.

Then he'll hit you with the killer fact: this wall is a retaining wall and carries the weight of all the floors and masonry above it.

The builder has completed the first step of the **FODA** process. He has gathered the facts and evidence. Now he needs to tell you what he has found and take you on to the second stage of the process. He will move on to explain the consequences of getting this job wrong.

Please note, he does not go straight to the solution and frighten you with a huge estimate for the job. It would be wholly inappropriate to do so at this stage of the consultation.

Instead, he will explore the consequences and opportunities of this information with you. By now, your beautiful vision of a light, open space at the heart of your home has just vanished in a puff of dust as, in your mind's eye, you see your entire house collapse after you've taken just one swing with that sledgehammer you were going to use. In just ten short minutes, the builder has taken you from a beatific dream to a householder's nightmare. He has helped you understand that the cost of getting this job wrong is not $300 but $300,000! It's called building the pricing context, and builders are very good at it.

So when the builder does eventually get around to telling you the price for doing this job correctly, you'll be judging that price against $300,000, not $300. But he's not got to that stage yet. He will now talk about the options, the opportunities, for getting this job done, and done right.

At this stage the builder, who, like all people in the professions, has his own set of technical language and terminology, will throw in lots of jargon. This is the only stage in the process where technical jargon is appropriate. Anywhere else it is just meaningless drivel and must be avoided at all costs. But this is the time to use it. Because it is now that the builder will specify what needs to be done.

The language the builder uses in this explanatory section will be technical. He will talk animatedly about the step-by-step process that has to be undergone in order to deliver the end result without compromising the integrity of the entire structure. He will go on and on about the different materials that could be deployed, the necessity of using RSJs, framed construction, beam-and-block floors, thin joint systems, masonry baton shells and a whole host of other obscure-sounding stuff that means nothing to you. Nor is it meant to, for the use of this technical language is to signal to you that you cannot do this and that you need an expert. So if you think he's just boring on and on with minutiae, and that he doesn't realize how dull all this is, you have missed the point. He's showing you that you need him.

And now he has taken you through this process, what has happened to your price expectation? It will be less than $300,000 but significantly more than $300!

Now the builder has got you thinking about the job in a realistic way, he will expand your desire to buy. From your opening description of what you want, he will have heard your desire to lay stripped-oak wooden floors. He will ask whether you will take up the existing carpet prior to any builders coming on to the site. You, being busy, will probably ask him whether his team would be able to take up the carpet and dispose of it. "And have you lined up the flooring material and a fitter for laying the oak floor when we're done?" he will enquire.

He's reminding you of the dream and repainting your vision of the end result, as if it's nearly realized. Again, you will probably not have got this far in your planning, so he will wait for you to ask whether he could help. He will say that he knows a very good floor fitter, but that this person is always booked up. But he'll see what he can do.

Then, and only then, will the builder specify the entire list of necessary actions and give you a price. And you know what, you'll actually be grateful to him, because he's done a good job taking you through the process of discovery that is top-level consultative salesmanship.

FODA works in your everyday dealings with clients

Quite often, clients call you up and ask whether you can help them out with an urgent request. They say that they are sorry to land this on you at the last minute, but their own boss has asked for a full analysis of the company's financial risk exposure on an acquisition they are looking to make which he wants to use in the board meeting this coming Monday. It is now Friday. Even though you know that your client, in this case the chief treasurer, has been aware that this would be needed for the past ten days, he has landed it on your desk with just seventy-two hours to go. As a loyal, keen client service professional, what is your immediate, knee-jerk reaction (albeit through gritted teeth)?

"No problem," you hear yourself say down the phone. And you work all through the weekend to deliver. The following week you send the invoice for this weekend work through, and the moment it arrives you get a call from an irate client.

"You said this was no problem. An invoice for twenty-five thousand dollars *is* a problem. I'm not paying this. You never mentioned this. If I'd known it was going to cost this much I'd have gone elsewhere."

What would the builder say if he was asked to do something last minute by a valued client and he worked at your company?

He'd say: "Let me just make sure I understand what you want." He'd repeat the brief. "Hmmmm. I *think* that

might be possible, but let me tell you what's involved."
He'd then talk about reallocating resources, taking people
off another important job in order to accommodate this
new urgent commission, having to negotiate with the
head of portfolio optimization in Corporate Solutions for
an analyst's time over the weekend. He would help the
client understand that this was a big ask. It wasn't "No
problem". And it would have a reasonable price tag
attached. In this way there are no nasty surprises and the
client still gets what he wants, but so do you.

17
Knowing when to ask for more business

They say that the secret of good comedy is timing. Timing is also an important factor in getting a client to say yes to your proposal. Judge the timing correctly and all your preparation and hard work leading up to the client meeting will bear fruit; get the timing wrong and the conversation can be over very quickly. Knowing when to ask is key.

When do you ask?

It strikes us that too many people wait until the end of a project to ask the client whether there's any other work they want them to do. There are other, much more effective times to strike. At the beginning of a new relationship or new project (which we covered in Chapter 7 – "we've only had the client a little while and we don't want to seem pushy") is ideal because the client will read your request as hunger, not avarice, and because you will be forgiven some gaucherie at the beginning of your relationship whereas you would be expected to know the rules once you're more established.

Halfway through a job is also a great time to ask what else you can be doing for your client. The reason for this is simple. Halfway through a job there is still an anticipatory sense of excitement and expectation. And as we all know, expectations are often superior to what eventually transpires. Halfway through a job, there are no unwelcome surprises, no unexpected costs, no larger-than-life invoices. The psychological buying mode halfway through is optimistic. There's a sense of full steam ahead – very unlike the swirl of unmet expectations and disappointment that *can* accompany the post-project atmosphere! So if you give them the **HEAT treatment** halfway through a job, you'll get a much more upbeat reaction – one that's riding the wave of the client's enthusiasm for working with you when everything is going swimmingly.

The HEAT treatment (hit 'em with another thought)

Think of it like this: if you've had a major birthday party at your home and you've hired outside caterers, how have you felt halfway through the party as compared with how you felt when all the guests had gone at the end? You feel very different at those times.

At the end of the party, there's that huge sense of anticlimax. Everyone has departed, the debris needs clearing away, the thank-you letters have to be written for the presents everyone bought you, one of your prized lamps was broken, and you have a suspicion you authorized the bartender to open twelve more bottles of champagne than you'd budgeted for … all in all, it's a headache, literally and metaphorically.

Contrast this with your mood earlier once the party was in full swing. You flitted from guest to guest, from group to group. The room was full and alive with the buzz of animated and convivial conversation. The catering staff were working the room immaculately, making sure that no one's glass was empty and that the canapés were circulating constantly. All your guests complimented you on a fantastic party and said that you were looking fabulous. Everyone was laughing and enjoying themselves. It was a great party. You were euphoric.

If you were the caterer, when would you make your approach to ask for more business?

The caterer will discreetly sidle up to you halfway through the party and ask you whether everything so far is to your satisfaction. Dazzled by the success of your party and high on the whole experience, you will affirm that everything is not just fine but superb. You will lavish praise on the caterer's staff and the food being served. At this point, the caterer will quietly ask you whether you have any plans for another such party nearer to the holiday season, later in the year. He asks this, he says, because his diary is already filling up and he wants to make sure that such a valued customer as you doesn't miss out. You say you hadn't really thought that far ahead, but yes, that might be a good idea. He nods and says that he will leave you alone to enjoy the rest of your party, but that he will call you on Monday to discuss any thoughts you have had on this event and to discuss your plans for the next one.

You have just had the **HEAT treatment.** Used judiciously and at the right time, it opens the door to potentially profitable conversations.

Tidy up time

Another tactically effective time to have a conversation about new initiatives is at the end of the week. People like lists. Especially at work. Time management courses teach the need to set objectives and goals, to prioritize those goals and to monitor progress on a regular basis. In other words, write a list of what you need to do, cross each item off your list as you do it and compile a new list for the following week. And most people seem to work one week at a time – that's their time frame for organizing their work life.

How can you use this priority-setting habit to advantage?

Monday is action day. People tend to get to their office and survey the workload they have for the week. It often feels like a fresh start – they can see five days ahead and they know what they've got to achieve. So go to it – Monday is the day to get your initiative on your client's agenda.

On Friday, they're in review-and-plan mode. What has been achieved? What can be crossed off the list? What is still hanging over to next week?

This compulsion to organize and tidy up our workflow

can be used to **get decisions from clients or to move closer to getting a decision.** On a Friday afternoon*, people are prone to making decisions – it just gets one more thing off their list. If you have a well-prepared argument making the case for taking action on an issue you've identified earlier then you have a higher probability of getting client commitment at a Friday afternoon meeting.

Even if the client says he needs to think more about the issue, or to discuss it over the weekend with a colleague, you can still move closer to a commitment by offering to call him on Monday when he's had a chance to consult and cogitate. If you're *really* disciplined, you'll go back to your office and send him a detailed email highlighting the factual evidence, spelling out the consequences and opportunities and specifying your recommended solution. Then you call him on Monday.

---

* Thursday afternoon in Arab culture.

Part 3 summary

Being more effective with your clients

Avoid the maturity rut: the basis of successful organic growth must be a strong relationship with the client. This means not just delivering the agreed services to the minimum (contracted) standards but ensuring that the relationship is vibrant and rewarding.

Spend the right time with the right people: the day with your clients in their office or their outlets can be infinitely more valuable than your day in your office.

Understand your clients and their professional style: be aware too of your own style and learn to adapt to that of others.

Think beyond today: analyse your clients' needs from new and different perspectives.

Every meeting needs a plan: use NISE and FODA to present your case in the most compelling manner at a time when the client has leisure to discuss it properly.

Questions are paramount: different questions will provide different types of answer. Use the right question to get the information you need.

Timing can help: now is better than tomorrow, earlier is better than later.

18
Take action now

If you want to change the results you're getting, you have to make the effort to change. We hope you will use the techniques and skills we've written about in this book, and we hope you enjoy making the effort and achieving the better results you will get when you do. And if you want the whole philosophy of what we're saying in a nutshell, here it is:

If you mean to profit, learn to please.
(W. S. Churchill)

ALSO BY DAVID KEAN

ISBN 978-1-905736-24-9

£7.99